Cognitive Computing

Dr. Arockiasamy Clementking,

PG and Research Department of Computer Science,

Don Bosco College, Guezou Nagar,

Yelagiri Hills. Vellore Dt, Tamil Nadu, India.

S. Rani,

Integrated Intelligent Research,

India.

Published by

BONFRING®
Intellectual Integrity

Cognitive Computing

9 789387 862302 >

ISBN 978-93-87862-30-2

Authors

Dr. Arockiasamy Clementking

S. Rani

Bonfring

309, 2nd Floor,

5th Street Extension, Gandhipuram,

Coimbatore-641 012.

Tamilnadu, India.

E-mail: info@bonfring.org

Website: www.bonfring.org

Phone: 0422 4213231

Author Profile

Dr. Arockiasamy Clementking is working as a faculty in PG and Research Department of Computer Science, Don Bosco College, Yelagiri Hills, India as well as serving as a Consultant for National Commission for Academic Accreditation & Assessment (NCAAA) in the kingdom of Saudi Arabia. He secured Doctor of Philosophy (Ph.D) in Computer Science from University of Madras, India and Doctor of Philosophy (Ph.D) in Computer Application from Bharath University, India. He served as a Consultant to Vice Rector Office for Academic Development and Quality, King Khalid University while serving as a faculty in the Department of Computer Science, King Khalid University, in the Kingdom of Saudi Arabia.

He contributed his knowledge for academic development in the field of Data mining to design Master Slave Back Propagation model to predict the Multi-variation on water Quality. He secured academic and research exposure in the field of Computer Science specialized with Data Mining Applications, Educational Mining, Cognitive Science, Medical Image Processing and Knowledge Engineering. He published more than 30 international and national journal publications in his research fields. He served as a reviewer for various Journals and resource person for various national and international conferences/seminar and workshops. He is one among the recognized trainer for quality system and accreditation practice for national and International accreditations.

With his self-learning, he equipped himself into higher educational quality assurance system and accreditation practices. He is serving as a team member and experts for preparation, review and consultant for national and international accreditation process. He has depth knowledge on various accreditation practices such as Accreditation Board of Engineering and Technology (ABET), USA, National Commission for Academic Accreditation & Assessment (NCAAA), Kingdom of Saudi Arabia, Saudi Qualification Frame Work (SQF), National Assessment and Accreditation Council (NAAC), India, National Board of Accreditation (NBA), India and National Institutional Ranking Framework (NIRF), India.

He taught core computer science Courses while working as a faculty in King Khalid University, Loyola College, Chennai; SRM University, Chennai; Sacred Heart College, Tirupattur; Kodaikanal Christian College, Kodaikanal and SIES College of Management Studies, Mumbai. However, he secured international exposure from the Salalah College of Technology, Oman as a Lecturer, and in the Ministry of Education. In addition to that from State of Eritrea, Department of HRD, Training and Development Division as an Information Technology trainer.

He learned management skills and practices as part his master degree on Personnel Management and Industrial Relationship (MA (PM&IR)) from Alagappa University as well as Post Graduate Diploma in Business Administration (PGDBA) from Pondicherry University.

With his exposure, he established a research center in India named as "Integrated Intelligent Research" (www.iirgroups.org) to serve young researchers and higher educational Institutions. He launched five international journals to facilitate research activities in the current trends. He is serving as a key members in IIR, India; KCS, Korea; SCIR, Thailand and ASSAR, UK.

He has vast academic and research exposure in the field of Computer Science and Applications along with organizing conferences and events for Research and Quality system.

S. Rani is a research scholar doing her doctoral degree in Computer Science, Presidency College affiliated to University of Madras. Previously she served as a faculty in the Department of Computer Science, King Khalid University, in the Kingdom of Saudi Arabia.

She secured academic and research exposure in the field of Computer Science specialized with Data Mining Applications in Medical Image Processing .She published her research findings in international and national journal in her research fields. She is serving as a reviewer for national and international Conferences. She is working as a managing editor IIR group of Journals.

Overview of the Book

Cognitive Computing is the replication of human thought processes in an automated model. Cognitive computing involves self-learning methods that use various techniques such as data mining, pattern recognition and natural language processing to imitate the way the human brain works.

Cognitive Computing plans to expand a logical, combined, universal mechanism stimulated for the mind's capabilities. The cognitive processes, which are of different types, are constructed by independent solutions. Rather than gathering it as a collection of piecemeal solutions, looking to execute a combined computational theory of the mind. Artificial Intelligence (AI) pioneer, Allen Newell, described it as "A single set of mechanism for all of cognitive behavior. Our crucial goal is a combined theory of human cognition." Traditionally, several diverse fields have fundamentally taken different approaches to appear in the mind-like computation, some of that are covered here. The AI takes a system-based approach to synthesize mind-like computers, and on the other hand, Neuroscience takes a system-based approach to know how it gives rise to minds, because the mind arises from the wetware of the brain. Cognitive Neuroscience seeks to combine Theoretical Cognitive Science with Experimental Psychology and Organism-Level Neuroscience when it proceeds from a top-down reductionist approach. Alternately, proceeding from the bottom-up in a constructive fashion, systems Neuroscience seeks to combine experimental data at multiple spatial and temporal scales.

Today, computing systems that can provide accurate, in-the-moment knowledge that lets to make strategic decisions across multiple fields such as science, legal, tax and finance.

A strategic decision that one has to make with respect to Cognitive Science is the level(s) of analysis (i.e., level(s) of abstraction) at which one models Cognitive agents. Computational Cognitive modeling can vary in terms of the level of process details and granularity of input and output, and as a result, is also carried out in multiple phases. We shall look into the issue of the multiple phases of Computational Cognitive modeling, drawing upon the work of Sun, Coward and Zenzen. We must be aware that the ordinary theories of multi degree evaluation considers there are various stages, each of which involves varying amounts of computational theory.

Cognitive model simulations of human behavior now perform tasks ranging in complexity-from simple mental arithmetic to controlling simulations of complex real-time computer-based systems, such as nuclear power plants. In the future, these models will become even more powerful and useful. Providing Cognitive models access to users' tasks can be done in three ways. In the first, the task simulation is implemented in the Cognitive modeling language. This is the best approach when the focus of the modeling is mainly on the internal cognitive aspects and when the task is quite simple. Numerous models have used this approach, (Newell and Simon, Peck and John, and Ritter et al.) In the second method, a simulation of the user's task is implemented in a simulation language; however, the interface or task cannot be directly used by human users, and the model's task simulation may not provide a visible representation of the task or of the model's behavior.

A cognitive device can provide real-time solutions to questions posed in natural language by way of looking through large numbers of statistics, which have been entered into its knowledge base, making feel of context and computing the maximum possible solution. As developers and customers "train" the system, the solutions become more reliable and increasingly treasured over the years.

An automatic system is being developed to disseminate information to the various sections of any industrial, scientific or government organization. This intelligence system will utilize data-processing machines for auto-abstracting and auto-encoding of documents and for creating interest profiles for each of the "action points" in an organization. Both incoming and internally generated documents are automatically abstracted, characterized by a word pattern, and sent automatically to the right action points. This book illustrates the flexibility of such a system in identifying known information, in finding who needs to know it, and in disseminating it efficiently, either in abstract form or as a complete document.

Cognitive Computing is the Central Nervous System (CNS) of the nascent crop of six ground-breaking technologies and products, forming the key factor to understand and perceive humans, things, events and the environment.

Imbued with the capacity to simulate human intelligence and effectually process ambiguous information and problems, Cognitive Computing can also be the key for data analysis and decision-making, undoubtedly. Cognitive systems are information systems that contain the cognitive hallmarks of learning, inferring, deducing, and computing.

Chapters	Contents	Page No
1	**INTRODUCTION TO COGNITIVE COMPUTING**	**1**
	1.1. What is Cognitive Computing	1
	1.2. The Origin of Cognitive Computing	2
	1.3. Define Cognitive Computing	4
	1.4. Cognitive Computing Users	4
	1.5. Cognitive System Algorithm and Applications	7
	1.6. Trends and Forecasting Research Pathway	15
	1.7. Cognitive Computing Environment and Circumstances	17
	1.8. Overview of Algorithm and Applications	17
	1.9. Application	20
	1.10. Summary	26
2	**APPLICATIONS AND BUILDING OF COGNITIVE COMPUTING SYSTEM**	**27**
	2.1. Introduction of Building Cognitive Solutions	27
	2.2. The History of Computing and the Rise of Cognitive Computing	28
	2.3. Cognitive Models	30
	2.4. Impacts of Knowledge Domain Modeling in Cognitive Systems	32
	2.5. Cognition and Programming	41
	2.6. Structure of Cognitive Computing Applications	44
	2.7. Summary	51
3	**COGNITIVE COMPUTING VS DATA ANALYTICS**	**52**
	3.1. Introduction	52
	3.2. Why Cognitive Analytics?	53
	3.3. The Benefits of Cognitive Analytics	53
	3.4. What to Do Now in Cognitive Analytics?	54
	3.5. How Does Cognitive Computing Relate to Analytics?	55
	3.6. Data Analytics of Cognitive Computing	57
	3.7. Big Data Analytics Adoption	58
	3.8. Why Cognitive Analytics?	66
	3.9. Summary	71

4	**MACHINE LEARNING AND COGNITIVE SYSTEMS**	**72**
	4.1. The Next Evolution of Enterprise Intelligence	72
	4.2. Business Intelligence and Big Data	76
	4.3. Machine Learning is a Reality for Business	79
	4.4. The Real Trouble with Cognitive Computing	80
	4.5. Thinking Big with Cognitive Computing	84
	4.6. Cognitive Computing as a Service	86
	4.7. Genetic Algorithms and Evolutionary Algorithms – Introduction	88
	4.8. Summary	90
5	**EMERGING EVOLUTION IN COGNITIVE COMPUTING APPLICATION**	**91**
	5.1. Affective Computing (AC)	91
	5.2. Analytics	95
	5.3. Artificial Neural Network	100
	5.4. Cognitive Reasoning	104
	5.5. Natural Language Processing	106
	5.6. Cognitive Computing Algorithm Application	107
	5.7. Social Neuroscience	109
	5.8. Synthetic Intelligence	110
	5.9. Summary	114

CHAPTER 1

Introduction to Cognitive Computing

1.1. What is Cognitive Computing

The aim of Cognitive Computing is to simulate human concept strategies in an automated model. It is defined as a Computing model to simulate human Cognition process to develop an effective and optimized solution for Complex real time problems. It embedded with Utilizing self-finding out algorithms that use information mining, pattern realization and usual language processing. The promising approach is to leverage large-scale computer simulations by processing huge collections of data model. To generate near real-time simulations at the scale of small mammalian brains, resources from Neurophysiology and Neuroanatomy are combined. Cognitive Computing are using various steps such as discovering, demonstrating and delivering the fundamental algorithms to gain a deep scientific understanding of how the mind perceives, thinks, and acts. It will lead to novel solutions. It can mimic the high-quality approach with which the human mind functions. While computing methods were more rapid at calculations and processing than humans for a very long time, they have not been capable to accomplish tasks that people take for granted as convenient, like understanding natural language, or recognizing specific objects in an image. Therefore the Cognitive computing approach attempted to mimic human solution using integrations of algorithms and model.

In cognitive programs, IBM Watson, rely on deep learning algorithms and neural networks to process working out through evaluating it to a learning set of know-how. The more understanding the process is exposed to, the more it learns, and the more accurate, it becomes over time, and the neural neighborhood is a problematic "tree" of selections the personal computing could make to reach at an answer.

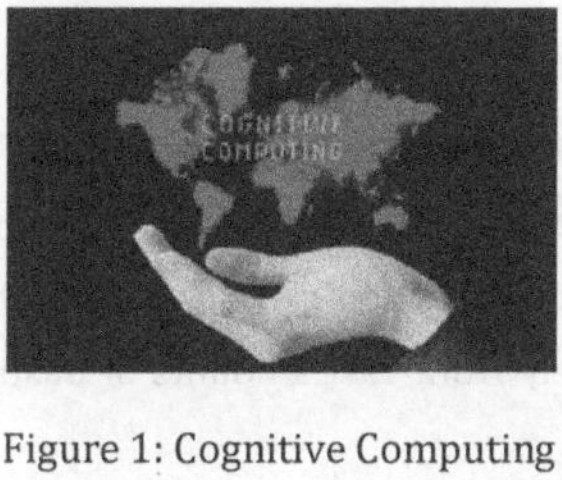

Figure 1: Cognitive Computing

Source:https://betanews.com/wp-content/uploads/2016/10/Cognitive-computing-e1476955448247.jpg

It is integrated system of computing architectures, programming paradigms, practical applications and business intelligent.

The Cognitive computing process will lead to provide the solution for all the day to day activities across the world. It will provide the solution based on expectation level, process and the understating of the assignment.

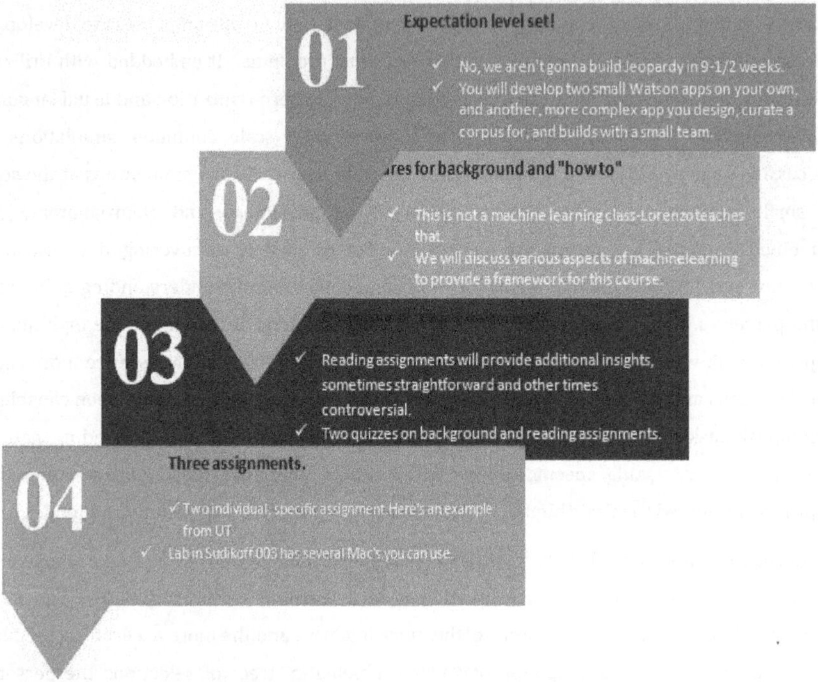

Figure 2: Introduction for Cognitive Computing

1.2. The Origin of Cognitive Computing

Cognitive programs are outlined by using a couple of traits to substitute than automate it. It will advise and provide evidence rather than produce a binary reaction for learning and strengthen as an alternative than stay static. To achieve better understanding of the field, cognitive programs gather closely from vast amounts of unstructured written content, voice, and image data.

The information is efficient, so that system can get the high value while providing high end real time solution with expected efficiency on the solutions.

New applied sciences such as program-defined storage and flash- established storage are the groundwork for the cognitive knowledge infrastructure. New cognitive workloads, reminiscent of deep learning and computer intensive. Cognitive processors are designed primarily for dealing with big data problems by offering infrastructure well suited to the latest analytic engines similar to Apache Spark.

Systems designed, above all, to fit specialized processors like Graphic Processing Units (GPUs) or Field-Programmable Gate Arrays (FPGAs) are becoming the standard for computationally-intensive training of cognitive programs.

Figure 3: Graphic Processing Units (GPU)

Source: http://www.neurdon.com/wp-content/uploads/2010/10/GPU.jpg

An FPGA is a built-in Circuit (IC) that may be programmed within the field after manufacture. FPGAs are alike in principle processor with wider potential application than Programmable Read-only Memory (PROM) chips.

FPGAs are utilized by engineers in the design of specialized ICs that can later be manufactured hard-wired in large quantities for distribution to computer manufacturers and end-users.

Eventually, FPGAs can enable PC users to modify microprocessors to meet their own individual requirement. *Advantages of using FPGA is listed below*

- Application-Specific Integrated Circuits (ASICs) and the market time is tremendously faster.
- The ability to execute high computing functionality beyond Application-Specific Standard Product (ASSP).
- Customizable and reprogrammable after the device has been deployed in the field.

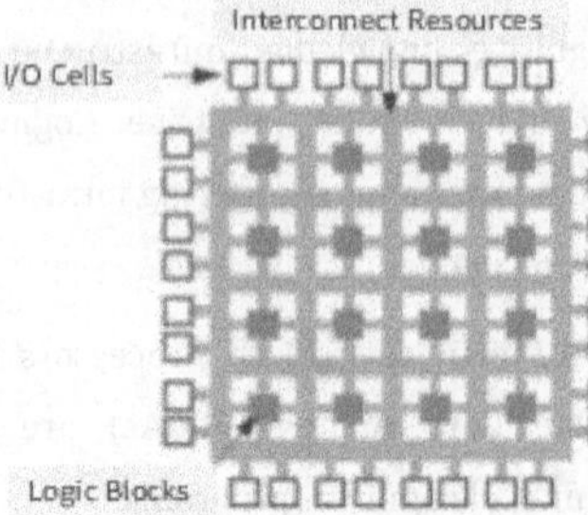

Figure 4: Field Programmable Gate Array (FPGA)

Source:https://image.slidesharecdn.com/dcws008-sf15dcws008100ffpga-151001124815-lva1-app6891/95/using-a-field-programmable-gate-array-to-accelerate-application-performance-12-638.jpg?cb=1443703761

1.3. Define Cognitive Computing

Cognitive computing is defined as an applied sciences that are based on the scientific standards of AI and signal processing, encompassing reasoning, machine learning, human-PC interaction, natural language processing, knowledge mining and more. It aims to solve complex problems implemented via uncertainty and ambiguity, which in other word implies problems that may be easily solved by way of human cognitive concept.

Cognitive Computing is defined as *the simulation of human thought processes in a computerized model. A cognitive system performs the cognitive work of planning, deciding, problem solving, analyzing, understanding, knowing, assessing, synthesizing and judging as they are fully integrated with perceiving and acting*.

1.4. Cognitive Computing Users

Some Main Cognitive Computing Companies are:

1.4.1. IBM

IBM Watson, built on Linux on Energy, is the embodiment of this new technology. It leverages deep content evaluation and proof-based reasons to accelerate and improve selections, reduce costs and optimize outcomes.

Watson makes use of a collection of transformational technologies, which leverage distinctive language; generate hypotheses and proof-based study. Combined with massively parallel probabilistic processing approaches, Watson can fundamentally change the way in which look at fixing issues speedily. Organizations are using business logics to discover imminent into their performance and identify future opportunities. Nevertheless, systems can also transform the way we think, behave and operate. In today's cognitive systems era, systems can learn through experiences, find correlations, create hypotheses, and remember and learn from the outcomes.

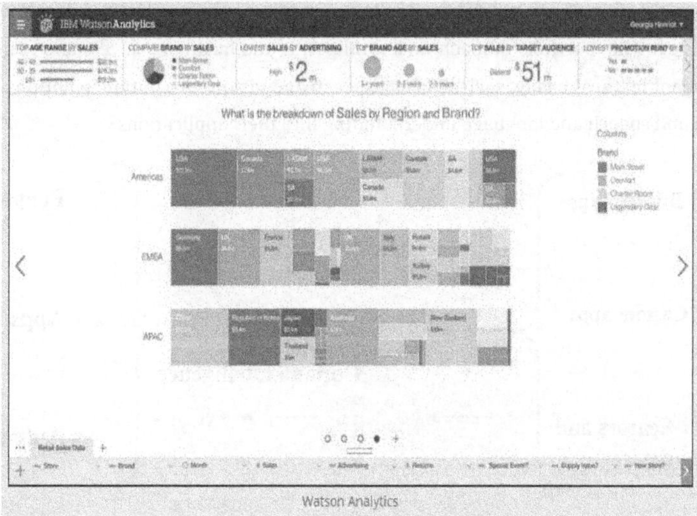

Figure 5: IBM Watson Solution

1.4.2. Microsoft

Microsoft develops, licenses, and supports a wide-range of software products, services and devices. The company's segments include more PC, Productivity and Business Processes. The company's products include Intelligent Cloud Operating Systems, server applications, business solution applications, desktop and server management tools, software development tools, cross-device productivity applications, video games, and training and certification of computer systems integrator and developer.

They also design, manufacture and sell devices including PCs, tablets, phones, entertainment consoles, gaming and other intelligent devices and related accessories, which integrate with its cloud-based services. It offers a range of services, comprising cloud-based solutions, which provide customers with software services, content and platforms, and it provides consulting services and solution support. It also provides online advertising to a global audience.

Microsoft Cognitive Services (formerly called as "Project Oxford") are a collection of APIs, Software Development Kits (SDKs) and services available to developers to make their applications extra smart, discoverable and engaging. Microsoft Cognitive Services develops on Microsoft's evolving portfolio of machine-learning APIs and facilitates developers to add smart and intelligent features easily, such as facial, speech and vision recognition; emotion and video detection; and speech and language understanding into their applications.

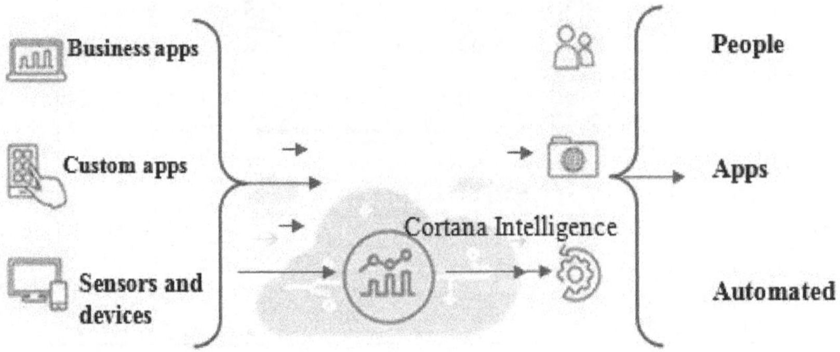

Figure 6: Microsoft Cognitive Computing

1.4.3. CISCO

Cisco Systems, Inc. are the global leader in networking for the Internet. At present, networks are a primary part of business, government, education and home communications. Cisco hardware program and service offerings are used to create the Internet Solution, which makes these networks viable, giving individuals, organizations and countries convenient access to knowledge and information, anywhere and at any time.

In addition, Cisco has pioneered the use of the Internet in its own trade practice and offers consulting services based on its expertise to support different organizations worldwide.

Cognitive Threat Analytics speedily detects and responds to attempts to establish a presence in your surroundings and to attacks which may be done or carried out or having started and in progress. All these are done without additional software or hardware to deploy.

Figure 7: Cisco Cognitive Computing

1.5. Cognitive System Algorithm and Applications

Cognitive Computing techniques is integration of understanding natural language, Adopt and learn and Generate and evaluate hypothesis. It can support human experts to make higher decisions by analyzing the complexity of large data.

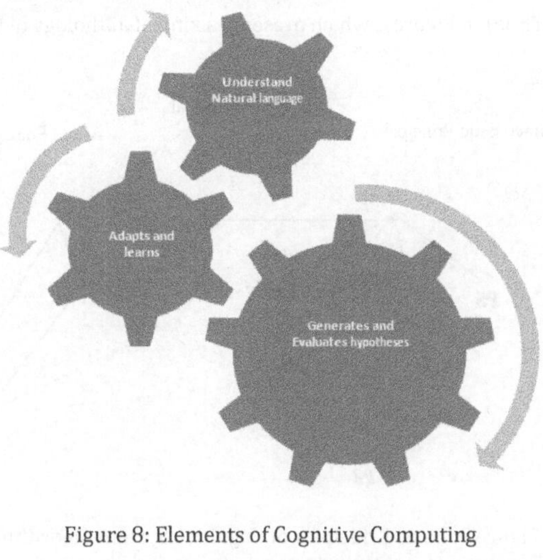

Figure 8: Elements of Cognitive Computing

Cognitive Computing process inspired by the functions and efficiency of the brain. The non-von Neumann nature of the TrueNorth architecture needs a novel technique to efficient system design. The abstractions and applications, which may be specifically effective for TrueNorth. IBM , First, developed repeatedly-used abstractions that span neural codes (such as rate, binary, time-to- spike and population), short-range connectivity and long-range connectivity. Second, executed 10 algorithms that comprise convolution networks, spectral content estimators, temporal pattern matching, liquid state machines, looming detection, restricted Boltzmann machines, hidden Markov models and various classifiers. Third, demonstrated seven applications, which include music composer recognition, speaker recognition, sequence prediction, optical flow, digit recognition, collision avoidance and eye detection. Their results highlight versatility, parallelism, spatio temporality, rich connectivity and multimodality of the TrueNorth architecture as well as the flexibility of the underlying neuron model and compositionality of the corelet programming paradigm.

1.5.1. Principles of Cognitive System Algorithm

The basic principles of different cognitive system algorithms can be split into two (i.e) characteristic and aided principles. Characteristic principles consist of ordering version space, hill-climbing principle, division of example space into subspaces, control with exceptions and competitive principle. Aided principles are: score function and reduction in the number of versions. Aided principles apparently join with characteristic principles. Combinations between various feature values are also possible. Possible combinations of all basic principles are presented (dash line) in Figure1, which presents a kind of anthology of basic principles.

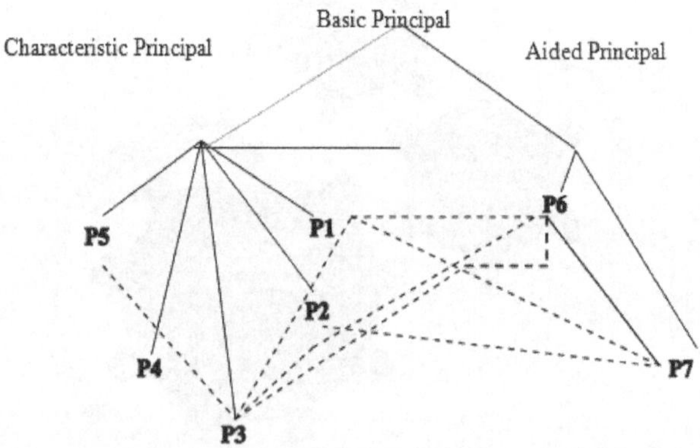

Figure 9: Basic Principles of Cognitive System Algorithm

In Figure 9: Basic Principles Ontology. (P1 - ordered version space, P2 – hill climbing principle, P3 - division of example space into subspaces, P4 - control with exceptions, P5 – competitive principle, P6-score function, P7-reduction of the number of versions).

A cognitive system is a distributed system in which people with diverse roles and capabilities, with the assistance of technological functions, collaborate in the planning and performance of cognitive work. Cognitive Computing techniques, gain knowledge, engage and adapt naturally with individuals to increase as well as combine the neutral capabilities of man and computer. They signify a contemporary and ongoing fusion of "sensible" heuristics, average language figuring out, artificial intelligence (AI) and what has turned out to be known as Human Headquartered Computing.

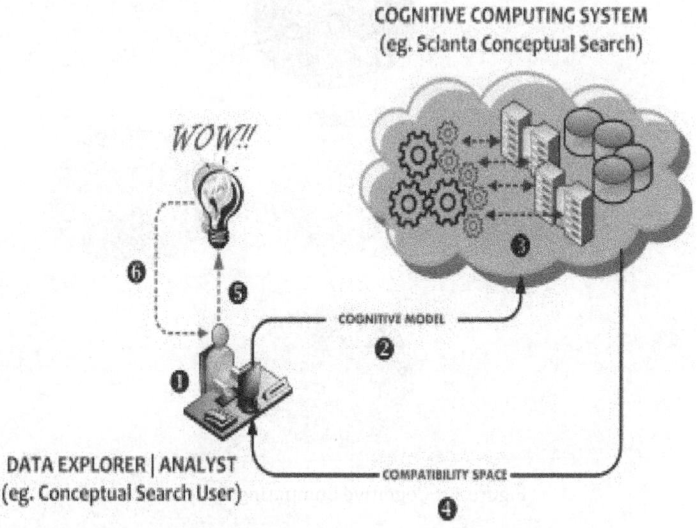

Figure 10: Cognitive Computing Systems

1.5.2. Cognitive Computing Systems

The Cognitive computing system are listed below

- Highly Integrated.
- Meaning-based.
- Theory of Probability.
- Iterative and Conversational.
- Interactive.

- Contextual.
- Big data knowledge based.
- Analytics.
- Learn and adapt based on interactions, new information, users.

Cognitive Computing denotes systems that learn at scale, reason with purpose, and interact with humans naturally. Instead of being explicitly programmed, they learn and interact naturally with people to extend what either humans or machines could do on their own. They help people to take better decisions by going through the complexity of big data.

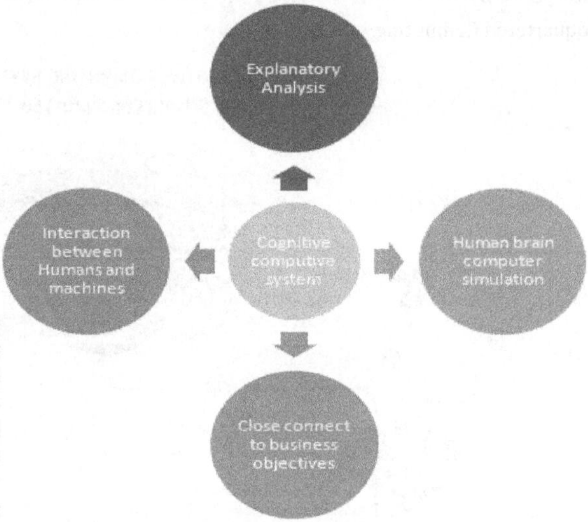

Figure 11: Cognitive Computing System

Cognitive Computing techniques are not programmed; they are informed to experience, predict, conclude and, in some methods, believe, utilizing AI and desktop-learning algorithms, which might be exposed to big data sets.

Scientists are pushing the boundaries of science and technology fields starting from nanotechnology to AI with the purpose of creating machines that do far more than calculate and prepare and in finding patterns in information they feel, learn, cause and interact naturally with persons in powerful new approaches. Watson's achievements on television had been one of the crucial first steps into a new phase within the evolution of information science the era of Cognitive Computing. The term Cognitive Computing is closely associated with IBM's cognitive computer techniques.

IBM Watson is a new computer approach that handles information processing in a different way than traditional computers. In a traditional example of computer systems a question perhaps is submitted to the computer to find, say, a name or quantity or knowledge on a particular area or thought. The computer then goes through the desk, or graph, and even the World Wide Web to find terms that fit what was searched. For example, say a chef is looking for innovative methods of cooking eggs. He could go into Google and search "Eggs Benedict." This question will show results such as the development of an egg, where it comes from, its importance in certain areas of the world, after which we get results about Saint Benedict, the movie "Benediction," and so forth.

With the intent to find the cooking method that is required, the very unique syntax is needed, and that would lead to results. With the combination of Cognitive Computing (CC), the PC utilized by a chef would fully grasp a question in phrases of context, which means, as it relates to the circumstance. In different phrases, it would give recipes for unique forms or variations of "Eggs Benedict" from various acclaimed cookbooks.

Cognitive Computing permits the computer to think about knowledge given in a basic manner. This enables the computer to grasp difficult and ambiguous suggestions and nuance inside the language. A remarkable accomplishment of these computers is their capability to fully grasp and interpret metaphors, similes, and idioms. Once more referring to the egg instance, cognitive desktops will possibly be able to recognize that the context of the search is coming from a chef. It is going to additionally keep in mind previous searches, which also had to do with food and cooking.

Then, after understanding the context and remembering previous searches, it sorts through the unstructured data, which is technology written or created by humans, for different people. Unstructured data includes blogs, microblogs (compared to Facebook or Twitter) news articles, and even videos - that is, possibly, most exceptional from classical computing, in that it focuses on unstructured knowledge. In keeping with IBM, as much as 80% of all knowledge in these days are unstructured.

1.5.3. Example for Cognitive Computing Systems

IBM Watson, Baby X, Google Now, Apple Siri and Microsoft Xiaoice are some of the examples of Cognitive Computing Systems that are capable of processing audio, videos and images to perform their respective tasks.

Let us take an example: It was just last year that Microsoft introduced Xiaoice, a chatbot, that has become a huge sensation in China.

People chat with Xiaoice when they have lost a job, or had nurtured a broken heart or have been feeling depressed. Since Xiaoice is not real, many people feel they can chat with her for hours, endlessly.

Others claim that she has a great sense of humor, exceptional listening skills and she gives and reciprocates the love.

People Communication with Xiaoice

According to the New York Times people who download Microsoft's Xiaoice app, enjoy talking to her. Irrespective of the fact that they are sad or happy, they talk with Xiaoice at least 60 times a month. Gao Yixin, a 24-year old, who works for an oil company stated, "When I'm in a bad temper, I'll chat with her."

Xiaoice Memory

People can add Xiaoice on main Chinese social networking services such as Web, a micro-blogging service provider used by seven-hundred million people, and Touch pal. Once they have added Xiaoice to chat on Chinese social networks, the users can have more in-depth chats with her.

Xiaoice Telling Jokes

"Xiaoice is a sophisticated conversationalist with a listing personality," wrote Microsoft on its Weblog.

It can chime into the conversation with facts about celebrities, sports, or finance, but also provides empathy and has a great sense of humor. Xiaoice recites poetry, tells ghost stories, repeats popular song lyrics, and knows a lot of jokes. When Xiaoice became really popular, she was telling more than 35.4 jokes per second on Weibo.

1.5.4. Algorithms in Cognitive Computing System

An algorithm is a procedure or formula for solving a problem based on conducting a sequence of specified actions. Algorithms may be expressed in many styles of notation, pseudocode, flowcharts, drakhon charts and programming languages.

Algorithm types that includes:

- Simple recursive algorithms.
- Backtracking algorithms.
- Divide and conquer algorithms.

- Dynamic programming algorithms.
- Greedy algorithms.
- Branch and bound algorithms.
- Brute force algorithms.
- Randomized algorithms.
- Simple sample Algorithm program.

  Step 1: Start.

  Step 2: Read the temperature in centigrade Step 3: store the value in C.

  Step 4: Set F to 32+ (9*C/5) Step 5: print value of C, F Step 6: stop.

1.5.5. Principles of Cognitive Computing Systems

Implications of the Cognitive Model for Instruction Five Foothold Principles The five principles of Cognitive Computing systems are:

a) The constructivism principle.
b) The context principle.
c) The change principle.
d) The individuality principle.
e) The social learning principle.

a) The Constructivism Principle

Principle 1: By creating networks with existing knowledge, the individuals can build their knowledge, so they use this knowledge by productively creating a response to the information they receive.

This principle summarizes the core of the fundamental ideas about the structure of long-term memory and recall. The basic mechanism of the cognitive response is context-dependent association. Several interesting results, illustrations and implications, which are pertinent for understanding and teaching Physics, approach from the constructivism principle.

b) The Context Principle

Principle 2: What people build depends on the context, including their mental condition.

The second principle reminds us of the non-uniqueness of cognitive response and sets the stage for a description of the dynamics of building mental structures.

It's very easy to disregard the warnings and drop back into the model that assumes students either know something or don't.

c) *The Change Principle*

Principle 3: It is quite easy to learn something that matches or extends an existing schema, but changing a fixed schema considerably is very difficult.

This principle deals with the dynamics of mental state. It states that schemas are not only the way that organize interactions with the world, but they also control how it incorporate new information and experiences [Bransford, 1973].

d) *The Individual Principle*

Principle 4: In learning, each individual is different from one another due to their mental responses and approach to learning.

This principle is called the individuality or the distribution function principle. This reminds us that several variables in human behavior have a large natural line width. The large standard deviation obtained in many educational experiments is not a trial error; it is part of the measured result!

In adding up to the information that students have diverse experiences and have drawn different conclusions from them, their methods of approach may differ significantly

e) *The Social Learning Principle*

Principle 5: In many individuals, mastering is most successfully finished via social interactions.

With the fifth principle, it go beyond single individuals and consider their relations to others as a division of their learning.

This principle is centered on the work of group learning that builds on the ideas of the Russian Psychologist, Lev Vygotsky.

These ideas have had a deep force on modern theories of teaching and learning The social mastering principle is mainly crucial for physicists to retain in mind. Physicists as a group are rather unusual in lots of approaches.

They learn to be in the intense tails of the distributions of curiosity, independence, and mathematical abilities.

1.6. Trends and Forecasting Research Pathway

The developing trend of growing cloud-established services, big data analytics and controlling the power of high-speed Internet has hugely added to the development of the Cognitive Computing market. The channel is sensing the gravitational pull of six most important technology traits - *Cloud Computing, mobility, Big Data, automation, Cognitive Computing AI, and the Internet of things (IoT).*

The report, "Global Cognitive Computing Market Measurement, Industry Analysis, Developments, Opportunities, Growth and Forecast, 2014-2020," stated that USA reported for the highest implementation of Cognitive Computing applications with a 41.6 % market share within the overall global revenue last 12 months. Within the coming 12 months, analysts count on these personal assistants to get much smarter, thanks to tendencies in machine learning out and Cognitive Computing. Asia-Pacific is anticipated to become a profitable market for Cognitive Computing. "In view that some of the applied sciences, underlying Cognitive Computing reminiscent of logistic regression, deep studying, and neural networks are already famous to analytics professionals."

1.6.1. How pervasive will Cognitive Computing become in the Next 10 to 20 Years?

(As written by James Kobielus in 2016).

In our physical life, Cognitive Computing will become physical artifact and also become part and parcel of our life over the next 10 to 20 years. The entire planet—and even the solar system and interstellar space-will be sensed, monitored, managed and optimized by cognitive IoT. As move deeper into the 21st century, humanity will deploy cognitive IoT across the universe as an extension of our organic nervous system, representing the realization of Arthur

Clarke's vision of "practical magic."

Humanity may even develop the long-sought (or long-feared) "master learning algorithm" by the middle of this century. By the way, here are few cognitive analytics industry predictions from a year ago, i.e., 2016:

- Cognitive analytics became inescapable in everyday life. Cognitive analytics are transforming life and work in the 21st century. Major trends include the implementation of cognitively-enriched intelligent machines such as Internet of Things (IoT) devices and mobile devices. The Cognitive Computing fabric will be interwoven into technology (for e.g. social media) and touch our everyday lives.

- Cognitive analytics has become the main focus of innovation. To drive business success, developers all over are building cognitive applications for every plausible use, and data scientists with cognitive skills are at the heart of this fast-emerging developer ecosystem.
- Cognitive analytics have begun to converge all big data Cognitive analytics, ingesting new types of data. The cognitive revolution runs on fresh feeds of an ever-growing pool of incongruent data, including IoT sensor data, media streams and other non-traditional sources.
- Cognitive analytics has become the hottest subject in data science. A new generation of data scientists are coming of age. These data scientists are experts in cognitive application development in Apache Hadoop, Apache Spark, R and other open tools and platforms. They are combining statistical modeling, programming skills and subject matter domain knowledge.
- Cognitive analytics will take root in global governance. As cognitive applications drive more business processes and automate decisions, society is calling for a wide-ranging legal, regulatory and policy structures to manage risks, compliance and implications.
- Cognitive analytics has become the principal personalization tool. Cognitive systems are becoming active, context-aware personalized interaction agents; the future of cognitive applications in our lives is pervasive personalization. Cognitive systems will increasingly understand the temporal and geospatial context of everything we do, and deliver responses that reliably fit for those contexts.
- Cognitive analytics has started to automate most data analysis. Cognitive systems are implementing unsupervised learning to automate sensing and detection of deep patterns and nuances within intricate data sets. Machine learning is facilitating automated systems to comprehend new concepts on their own and train themselves to be specialists.
- Cognitive analytics will drive further scaling in cloud data services. Cognitive systems are scaling indefinitely and inexorably. As Cognition-as-a-Service offerings such as IBM Watson gain implementation, the scalability will expand in the velocity, volume and variety of data and algorithms being implemented along with the resource requirements.

1.7. Cognitive Computing Environment and Circumstances

A cognitive environment is a communicating method occupied by the society of mechanisms and the devices that allow them to perform as one shared integrated resource, enabling "human-computer collaboration at the speed of thought."

Cognitive Environments can look and feel very different (from decision rooms in the workplace, to cars, to homes, to mobile), but by being connected to each other they will feel smooth. IBM has a research infrastructure (the Cognitive Environments Laboratory, known as the CEL) where they develop and refine the building blocks of Cognitive Environments. The CEL allows them to explore real-world use cases through testing and innovation with clients.

The applications include speaker recognition, chatboats, music composer recognition, machine translator, digit recognition, robotics, sequence prediction, health care, collision avoidance, automotive industries, cognitive radio, optical flow, communication, transport and vehicular detection, real time surveillance and eye detection. Demonstrating the scalability of TrueNorth, the systems used for these applications range in size from 38 to 3:1_106 neurons, 122 to 14_106 synaptic connections, and 1 to 21_103 cores.

The above-mentioned applications demonstrate the inherent parallelism and versatility of architecture, the ability of architecture to support spatial, temporal, and spatial-temporal processing, as well as, event-driven sensors; the architecture's ability to support representative inputs such as voice, music, images, text, and video; the richness and diversity of intra-core connectivity; the compositional power of the programming paradigm; and the flexibility of the neuron model presented in fig 12.

1.8. Overview of Algorithm and Applications

The algorithms and its concepts are presented below:

Convolution Network

Input to this corelet is sent to a bank of convolution filter corelets, where it is divided into16_16 patches, and each patch sent to a filter module corelet. A filter module corelet contains a single core whose neurons have receptive fields that individually represent a filter at a particular input location, and collectively apply an optimal convolution of input to the desired filter and thereby convolves horizontal, vertical and two-diagonal edge extraction kernels of dimension 3_3 each with the input image. Output from a convolution filter corelet is sent to an averaging corelet, containing cores configured to do an average-and-down sampling operation.

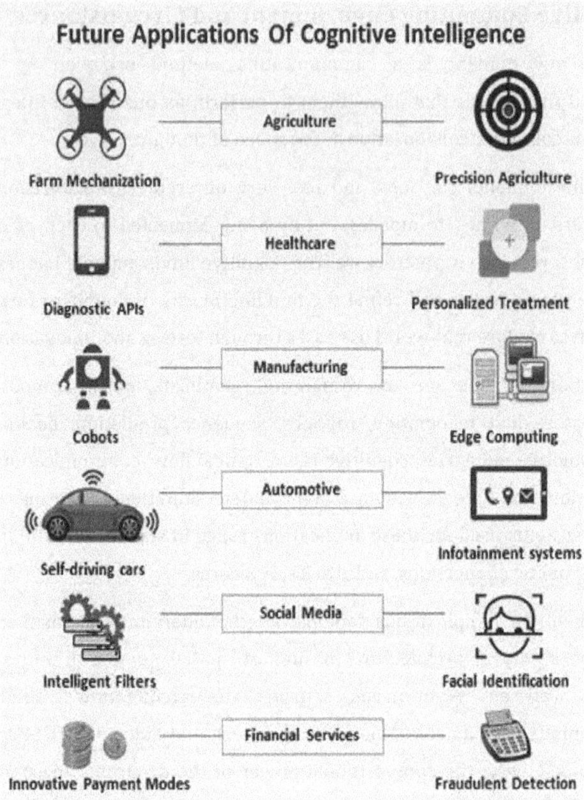

Figure 12: Future Applications of Cognitive Intelligence

Spectral Content Estimator

Input to this corelet is dispatched to a rectangular-wave filter out sub-corelet that implements a bank of square-wave filters with a configurable range of frequencies. Each square wave is separated into positive and negative components, further divided into 256 sample segments, and a neuron is configured with a receptive field matching each segment. These neurons, thus, compute a portion of the total dot product of the input with a square wave. In the summation corelet, a core collects all partial dot products for the same square wave. A single neuron is configured to sum the inputs, assigning a negative weight to inputs representing negative wave components and a positive weight to inputs representing positive wave components. The rate-coded output of a summation neuron, thus, represents the dot product of the input signal and the entire square wave.

Liquid State Machine (LSM)

LSM has introduced the process of searching for computational models that can help us to understand computations that are carried out in a "cortical microcircuit," i.e., in a local circuit of neurons in the neocortex (say in a "cortical column"). This approach has turned out to be quite successful since it made it possible to carry out quite demanding computations with circuits consisting of reasonably realistic models of biological neurons ("spiking neurons") and biological synapses ("dynamical synapses"). Note that in this model a large number of different readout neurons can learn to extract different information from the same circuit. One concrete benchmark task that has been considered was the classification ("recognition") of spoken digits.

Hidden Markov Model (HMM)

Hidden Markov models are used in most current research systems, because this technique produces better results for continuous speech with moderate-size vocabularies. The Hidden Markov models are stochastic state machines which combine probabilities of producing sounds with transitions from state to state. Best HMM models speech with the equal variations that arise in human speech owing to co-articulation and different consequences. Speech generated by a human being is coordinated against an HMM by computing the probability that the HMM would have generated the same sound or by finding the state sequence during the highest probability of producing the sound HMM. The fact that HMMs generate poor-quality speech explains why recognition based on HMMs is still not perfect. The sidebar "Hidden Markov models" further details the utilization of HMMs. Markov chains, although known about for almost a century, have only been successfully used in the background of speech recognition for the past 15 years orso.

Looming Detector

This correlate uses input from the motion-extraction correlate to compute looming for each pixel, a measure of how fast the object is expanding in the field of view. This model is inspired by the locust, which has dedicated looming neurons that it uses to detect potential collisions. Four partial looming subcorelets are used, each configured to compute one of the partial-looming signals R, L, U, or D for each pixel by using a neuron to sum the outward motion signals from two 3_5 flanking patches.

If this summation is positive, it is consistent with an expansion of an object in the field of view and if negative, it is not consistent and is ignored. Mathematically, this can be represented as,

$$Ls(x;y) = \max(0; \sum_{ij=-5}^{-1} ls(x+j; y+i) - rs(x+j; y+i));$$

Where rs and ls represent the rightward and leftward motion signals for speeds at a given pixel. Similar equations can be derived for the top, right and bottom windows. The final looming signal for each pixel is determined in a looming summation corelet, using neurons configured to compute.

$$S=1\ Rs + Ls + Us + Ds$$

Optical Flow

Optical flow is the apparent motion of objects in a scene relative to an observer, often described as the direction and magnitude of motion of each pixel in a frame. In a cognitive system, optical flow can play an important role in object tracking and navigation. Given two successive frames from a video, built a system that finds local changes in image edge locations as a measure of motion.

Optic flow denotes the image motion of the environment projected on the retina during our movement in the world. The term was first invented by James.J. Gibson, an American psychologist in the field of "Visual Perception," and played a crucial role in the development of the ecological approach to visible notion, a method that emphasizes analyzing human notion inside the natural environment instead of in a controlled laboratory environment. Considering the fact that James Gibson proposed that optic flow field consists of cues for the observation and management of self-movement, a lot of research in Cognitive Psychology and Neuroscience has investigated what precise cues from optic flow that humans use for the perception and control of self-movement.

1.9. Application

A. Speaker Recognition

Speaker recognition has been useful mostly in buildings and indoors of homes for security purposes as the device to control access or information exchange. One of the definite-type example is Texas instrument in the computer center security system. The capacity to process and combine information from a couple of sensors is the exclusive characteristic of cognitive \systems. It also provides the mechanism to limit the remote access of a personal workstation for a user or a set of registered users. It is used as a security device. Moreover, it helps to decrease the turnaround time on financial transactions in telephone initiated transfer of money. It provides extra security and verification as an added advantage.

Speaker recognition limits the access to information to authorized field people. In the security device, it is used to trigger specialized services based on a user's identity. In computer, it has limited applications of data using text independently.

Speaker recognition by computer has only had limited success to date in applications using free text (text-independent). Nonetheless, written content-unbiased reputation of speakers has grown to be a more and more popular area of study, particularly for programs including forensic intelligence accumulating and passive surveillance of voice circuits. Free-text reputation commonly lacks control over situations that influence machine performance, which includes variability within the speech sign, and distortions and sound inside the communication channel. The recognition task faces a couple of issues; unconstrained input speech, uncooperative audio system, and out-of-control environmental parameters. This has made it necessary to focus on the features of speech unique to the individual.

B. Music Composer Recognition

The common approach to tackling the composer identification and classification problem is through music theory and involves symbolic or score element analysis, which is done by musicians or musicologists, such as musical motif recognition, musical note durations and interval analysis.

The main domain in computer music data extraction is based on statistical refinement through the wave forms of musical pieces. Music content processing becomes an important domain of research. A lot of work regarding these tasks was published. It results from the fact that there are more and more repositories of a musical content available on the Web accessible for everybody.

Meanwhile, the tools for searching and browsing the text content, such as Google, were developed and are widely used. These tools were founded on the basis of IR (Information Retrieval) and NLP (Natural Language Processing). While it was found that people started to create music concurrently with language development, one can assume that music is also a natural language with all repercussions. This implies that some techniques with proven effectiveness in NLP and IR can be applied to the music as well.

C. Handwriting Recognition

Handwriting recognition is the ability of a computer to receive and interpret intelligible handwritten input from sources such as paper documents, photographs, touch-screens and other devices.

The image of the written text may be sensed "off line" from a piece of paper by optical scanning (optical character recognition) or intelligent word recognition. Alternatively, the movements of the pentip may be sensed "on line," for example, by a pen- based computer screen surface, a generally easier task as there are more clues available. Handwriting recognition principally entails optical character recognition; however, a complete handwriting recognition system also handles formatting, performs correct segmentation into characters and finds the most plausible words.

Recognizing and labeling symbols from noisy sub symbolic data is an essential capability for cognitive systems.

Given handwritten digits (0–9) from the MNIST dataset, a TrueNorth program to recognize and classify these images was developed. This task is challenging due to variation among writing styles, even among writing instances from the same person repeatedly writing the same digit. To overcome this challenge, a Restricted Boltzmann Machine (RBM) is used, which is a generative and unsupervised learning algorithm that clusters and extracts features from the data. This ability to cluster data into similar sets without using labels is appropriate to deal with the variations in writing styles, reducing the burden on the classifier.

The system comprises an RBM-trained feature corelet that extracts image features and sends them to a stochastic gradient descent trained linear classifier corelet that identifies the digit. Convolutional Neural Network (CNN) is the state-of-the-art solution for object recognition, and presents a workload that is both computed and data intensive. To reduce the workload, system train a shallow CNN offline, achieving 99.07% top-1 accuracy and utilize preprocessing and segmentation to reduce input image size fed into CNN. For CNN implementation of the mobile platform, it adopt and modify Deep Belief SDK to support batching fully-connected layers. On NVIDIA SHIELD tablet, the application processes a frame and extracts 32 digits in approximately 60ms, and batching the fully-connected layers reduces the CNN runtime by another 12%. Accuracy – less than 1% error rate.

D. Simple CNN Architecture

Compared with the state-of-the-art deep CNNs, which are designed for complex object recognition, it build a shallow network with fewer kernels and train it just for hand-written digit recognition.

The simple CNN requires much less memory and runs fast on mobile, and yet our result shows that it can still achieve similar outcomes.

By Construction, CNNs are Well Suited for Image Classification

- From one convolutional layer (CL) to the next, only a few units are connected together, which allows local treatment of subsets of pixels.
- Parameter sharing in one given CL contributes to the translational invariance of the model.
- In practice, the two constraints listed above drastically reduce the number of model parameters to be computed, and then allow training quite complex models in reasonable time.

A basic CNN consists in successions of convolutional layers (CL) and pooling layers (PL). Convolutional layers allow extracting several feature maps from the input images, while pooling layers perform some subsampling (i.e. dimensionality reduction) on the feature maps. Those successions of CLs and PLs correspond to a step of feature extraction.

For image classification, the output layer is a fully connected NN layer with a number of units equal to the number of classes. The output layer activation function is a softmax, so that the output unit activation is consistent with the probability that the image belongs to a class.

It's also common to see in a CNN, the CLs and PLs being combined with some rectification (non-linearities) and normalization layers that can drastically improve the classification accuracy (Jarrett et al. (2009))

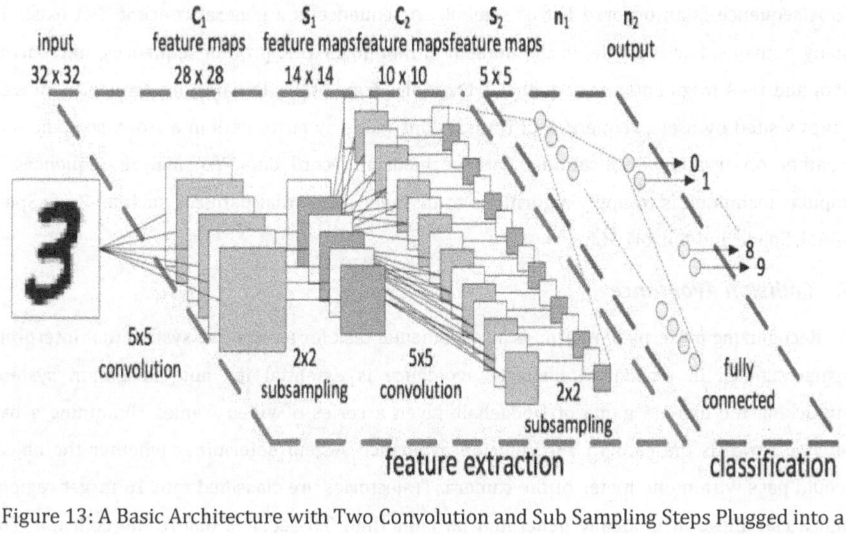

Figure 13: A Basic Architecture with Two Convolution and Sub Sampling Steps Plugged into a Classifier

Digit Recognition Using CNN

After the digit segmentation, the original image is slided and rescaled into 32*32 image patches of individual digits. The patches are fed into a CNN also for recognition. A custom CNN architecture, consisting of two convolutional layers (C1 and C2), two max pooling layers (S1 and S2) and two fully-connected layers (n1 and n2), as depicted in Figure 13. The output of F2 is passed to a 10-way softmax, which produces a probability distribution over ten labels (i.e. '0'-'9').

The first convolutional layer (C1) filters the 28*28 input grayscale image with 8 kernels of size 5*5, while the second convolutional layer (C2) filters the down-sampled 10*10*8 feature maps with 16 kernels of size 5*5*8. Both convolutional layers use a unit stride. Down-sampling occurs at layer S1 and S2 by applying 2*2 non-overlapping max pooling. The dimensions (e.g. convolution windows size, layer counts, kernel counts, etc.) of the network are similar to LeNet-5, which is an early CNN for handwritten digit recognition, though it use one less fully-connected layer. However, simpler yet more popular components to construct the network. For example, Rectified Linear Unit (ReLU) nonlinear function is used at the output of the conventional and fully-connected layers, which is much efficient to compute than the sigmoid or the hyperbolic tangent functions and also proved to be trained faster for the same accuracy.

E. Sequence Prediction

A sequence is an ordered list of symbols. A sequence is a general concept that exists in many domains. For example, in the domain of Bioinformatics, protein sequences, microarray data and DNA fragments are sequenced. Examples from other domains are sequences of web pages visited by users, sequences of transactions made by customers in a store, sequences of weather observations, educational data or medical record data. To analyze sequences, a popular technique is to apply algorithms to discover sequential patterns such as PrefixSpan, SPAM, Spade and Apriori ALL.

F. Collision Avoidance

Recognizing patterns of motion is a fundamental task for a cognitive system that interprets visual signals. In particular, obstacle avoidance is essential for any navigation system. Mimicking the age-old game of Dodgeball, given a series of video frames containing a ball moving towards the camera, the collision avoidance system determines whether the object would pass within one meter of the camera. Trajectories are classified into 16 target regions and a classification is ideally generated no later than 0.5 seconds before the collision. The collision avoidance system consists of four corelets: motion extractor, looming detector, feature extractor and nonlinear classifier. Motion Extractor: This corelet receives transduced spikes from each input pixel, split 16 ways with appropriate delays to enable the parallel computation of the motion signal for four speeds and four directions per speed. The corelet contains spatio-temporal filter sub-corelets, each with neurons configured to receive connections from three pixels, sampled from three video frames, for a total of nine inputs per neuron. Using a spatio-temporal filtering model as described, for example, in the summation carried out by the neuron coding the horizontal motion signal for velocity v at the pixel P located at row y, column x, for frame t is given by ,

$$Mot(x, y, t, v) = P(x, y; t-2) - P(x+v, y, t-2) - P(x+2v, y, t-2) - P(x, y, t-1) + P(x+v, y, t-1) - P(x+2v, y, t-1) - P(x, y, t) - P(x+v, y, t) + P(x+2v, y, t).$$

Here v = 1; 2; 3; 4 represents the velocity of the motion for rightward, and v = -1;-2;-3;-4 for leftward motions. A similar formula is used for vertical motion. Thus, the rate coded output of a single neuron represents the level of the motion signal for a specific speed, direction, and location.

G. Eye Detection

The ability to detect and track spatio-temporal patterns is a useful feature of cognitive systems. Given an on-axis and off-axis light source, it constructed a system that uses retro reflection to detect and track eye location, drawing inspiration. When an eye is illuminated, it reflects a narrow beam of light directly towards the light source. In flash photography, this reflection causes the undesired red eye effect; however, can be used advantageously for eye detection.

An on-axis light induces the red-eye reflection, producing an image with bright pupils, while an off-axis light results in a similar image, but with dark pupils. Subtracting the two images provides the location of the eyes. The iniLabs DVS128 spiking retina sensor instead of a traditional camera. This sensor has 128_128 detectors, or pixels, each spiking asynchronously when the change in light brightness exceeds a threshold. Each pixel may spike up to 1000 times a second, and the entire sensor can deliver up to two million spikes per second. The spikes are fed into our eye detection system, composed of a convolution and temporal integration corelet followed by an eye centroid detection corelet .

Eye Centroid Detection: The eye centroid detection corelet is composed of winner-take-all corelets. Each such corelet receives an 8_8 region from the convolution and temporal integration corelet, applies a filter to find the centroid of activity in the region, and outputs a single pixel, where the maximum activity is found.

1.10. Summary

In this chapter,

- The introduction of Cognitive computing and its origin are briefly explained.
- Cognitive computing is the simulation of human thought processes in a computerized model.
- Cognitive computing involves self-learning systems that use data mining, pattern recognition and natural language processing to mimic the way the human brain works.
- Real-world applications - The companies using cognitive computing such as IBM, MICROSOFT and CISCO. The system that proved a computer can learn, think and understand like a human.
- Building of cognitive computing system, and its algorithm and applications will be discussed in the next chapter.

CHAPTER 2

Application and Building of Cognitive Computing System

2.1. Introduction of Building Cognitive Solutions

Cognitive Computing represents a new generation of computing systems that are built to augment, accelerate, and scale human expertise, enabling a new era of genuine human-machine collaboration. Cognitive computing systems as systems that are able to understand, reason, and learn. In other words, systems that can determine meaning from data inputs structured and unstructured, text-based, or sensory by interpreting context and classifying the data as information, or knowledge.

To reason, these systems use data inputs and established understanding to form hypotheses, consider arguments, and prioritize suggestions. These systems are capable of continuous learning, accumulating data and insight through human interactions. Cognitive systems are not programmed, but are instead trained, acquiring knowledge through experience and improving with time.

Human interaction and partnership are central to both the technology and philosophy of Cognitive Computing. Earlier expert systems required hardcoded rules and decision trees that could supply only the answers to previously identified questions. Cognitive systems build on the knowledge, and learn a domain's terminology, processes and patterns of interaction through communication with human experts. These systems are not programmed, but pose hypotheses based on data patterns and probability. In turn, cognitive systems can then make recommendations, provide insights, and suggest discoveries.

2.1.1. To Enable Natural Human Interaction with these Systems

1. Image and speech recognition.
2. Deeper understanding of text.
3. Emotion detection and expression.
4. Translation tools.
5. Relation extraction.

These capabilities help with the understanding of actions between entities and the understanding of individuals and their specific communication needs. Cognitive systems also use visual analytics and data visualization techniques. These techniques display data in visually-compelling ways and do not rely on language only to be understood, but also graphic communication.

Color, tone, language, and mathematical figures are all ways in which Watson can understand and make itself understood. These systems fundamentally understand, reason, learn, and interact with humans naturally. In short, cognitive technologies make bigger human cognition -- assembling tremendous scales of disparate knowledge sources, reasoning through domain -specific inquiries, and obtaining new learning via expertise.

The system can then extract from its knowledge stores, ascertain connections that inform discoveries, and interactively guide decision making, entirely in a continuous feedback loop of human interaction and partnership.

2.2. The History of Computing and the Rise of Cognitive Computing

To better understand the future of Cognitive Computing, it is vital to place it in historical perspective. Up till now, there have been two distinct eras of computing, the Tabulating Era and the Programming Era, and IBM has played a major role in the development of both these eras. Cognitive Computing is the third and most transformational phase in computing's evolution. (Image1)

2.2.1. The Tabulating Era (1900s - 1940s)

The delivery of computing consisted of single-rationale mechanical techniques that counted, utilizing punched playing cards to input and store data, and to finally educate the computing device what to do (albeit in a primitive way). These tabulation machines have been almost calculators that supported the scaling of each business and society, serving to us to arrange, fully grasp, and manage the whole thing from population development to the advancement of a world economic climate.

Figure 14: Tabulating Era

Source:https://media.licdn.com/mpr/mpr/shrinknp_800_800/AAEAAQAAAAAAAAOrAAAAJDlhMWE3Y2E0LWQ1ZjMtNDM0MS1hYzIyLTA2YjRjYTJhYWFhMg.png

2.2.2. *The Programming Era (1950s - Present)*

The shift from mechanical tabulators to electronic techniques started during World War II, driven through navy and scientific needs. Following the war, digital "desktops" developed rapidly and moved into businesses and governments. They carried out if/then logical operations and loops, with instructional materials coded in software. Initially built around vacuum tubes, they were given a huge boost by the invention of the microprocessor and the transistor, which came to demonstrate "Moore's Law," doubling in size and speed every 18 months for six decades. Everything recognize as a computing gadget from the mainframe to the personal computer, to the smartphone and tablet is a programmable PC.

2.2.3. *Cognitive Modeling*

Cognitive models are appearing in all fields of cognition at a rapidly increasing rate, ranging from perception to memory to problem solving and decision-making. Over 80% of the articles appearing in major theoretical journals of Cognitive Science involve cognitive modeling.

1. Furthermore, applications of cognitive modeling are beginning to spill over into other fields including human factors, Clinical Psychology, Cognitive Neuroscience, Agent-Based Modeling in Economics, and many more.
2. Thus, cognitive modeling is becoming an essential tool for Cognitive Science in particular and Social Sciences in general, and any serious student with an inclination toward theory development needs to become a competent reader and perhaps user of these tools. To get a quick idea about cognitive models, here is a briefly described example. One highly active area of cognitive modeling is concerned with the question of how it learn to categorize perceptual objects. For example, how does a radiologist learn to categorize whether an x-ray image contains a cancerous tumor, a benign tumor, or no tumor at all?

How does a naturalist learn to categorize wild mushrooms as poisonous, edible, or harmless but inedible? How does an amateur art enthusiast learn to categorize paintings as belonging to the renaissance period, or romantic period, or modern period or some other period? One cognitive model is called the prototype model of categorization. Consistent with this model, the learner evaluates the focal tendency from the examples experienced from each category during the training. When a brand new target stimulus is displayed, the similarity of this target to each class prototype is evaluated, and the class with probably the most similar prototype is chosen. A different cognitive model is known as the exemplary model of categorization. In line with this model, the learner memorizes all the examples that are experienced from each and every class in the course of training. When a new target stimulus is displayed, the similarity of the target to each stored example is computed for each class, and the class with the highest total similarity is chosen.

2.3. Cognitive Models

The above examples illustrate what view as cognitive items; however what makes these units cognitive units as opposed to a few different variety of units, similar to conceptual items, or statistical units or neural models? Cognitive Science is concerned with figuring out the tactics that the brain, chiefly the human brain, uses to achieve complex duties together with perceiving, finding out, remembering, thinking, predicting, inference, problem-solving, resolution making, planning, and moving around the environment. The goal of a cognitive model is to scientifically provide an explanation for one or more of these basic cognitive procedures, or give an explanation for how these tactics interact.

2.3.1. Advantages of Cognitive Models

The major potential of cognitive models over conceptual frameworks is that, via making use of mathematical or computer languages, cognitive models are guaranteed to produce logically valid predictions. This is not genuine of conclusions established on intuitively-centered verbal reasoning. For example, early group researchers argued in favor of a prototype hypothesis overanexemplarhypothesisonthebasisofthefactthataprototypestimulus, which was never experienced during training, was categorized more accurately than a training stimulus, on a subsequent delayed transfer test. However, to group researcher's surprise, once the exemplar model was mathematically developed and tested, it was shown that their logic was incorrect, and the exemplar model could easily account for superior performance to the prototype stimulus. In this case, reasoning from a conceptual framework led to incorrect conclusions about evidence for or against competing theories of group learning.

2.3.2. Practical Uses of Cognitive Models

There are several practical uses for cognitive models in a wide-range of areas. Clinical psychologists use cognitive models to assess individual differences in cognitive processing between normal persons and clinical patients (for example, Schizophrenics). Cognitive neuroscientists use cognitive models to comprehend the psychological function of different brain regions. Aging researchers use cognitive models to comprehend the aging process and the slow-down or deterioration of cognitive functioning with age. Human reasoning researchers use cognitive models to improve human-machine or human-computer interactions. Decision researchers use cognitive models of decision making to predict preferences for purchaser products, investment portfolios for companies, medical picks, and military methods. AI and Robotic researchers use cognitive models for automatic detection of unsafe targets, automatic recognition of handwriting, automated recognition of faces, or avoidance or approach movement behavior of robots. Researchers in Social Science such as Economics and Sociology use cognitive models to construct computerized agents in agent-based items of market behavior or social networking.

2.3.3. Steps of Cognitive Modeling

The first step is to take a conceptual theoretical framework, and reformulate its assumptions right into a more rigorous mathematical or PC language description. Do not forget, for example, the prototype model that was in brief sketched earlier. To formulate the prototype for every class as a vector of points, and write down formulas describing how to compute the space between the target stimulus vectors and the prototype vectors. This first step uses the basic cognitive ideas of the conceptual conception to assemble the model.

In general the conceptual idea is inadequate or too weak to wholly specify a model, or it is missing very important details. In this case, the second step is to make additional detailed assumptions with a purpose to complete the model. That is customarily crucial for producing distinct quantitative predictions. For example, considering the prototype model, that need to make detailed, but somewhat adhoc assumptions about what features should be used to represent the stimuli to be categorized. Theorists attempt to scale back the number of ad hoc assumptions; however, this step is usually unavoidable. Models quite often include parameters, or coefficients that are initially unknown, and the third step is to estimate these parameters from one of the crucial found data. For example, the prototype model could comprise weight parameters that check the significance of each and every function for the categorization problem. The significant weight assigned to each and every function is a free parameter that is estimated from the choice response data. Theorists try to decrease the quantity of model parameters, but that is on the whole an essential and major step of modeling. The fourth step is to evaluate the predictions of competing models with respect to their capacity to provide an explanation for the empirical outcome. It is meaningless to ask if a model can fit the info or not. In fact, all models are intentionally constructed to be easy representations that best seize the necessities of the cognitive programs. Consequently we know, a priori, that each one unit is wrong in some details, and an adequate quantity of knowledge will continuously prove that a model will not be true. The question we have got to ask is which model presents a greater representation of the cognitive procedure that are trying to represent? For example, all know from the starting that both the prototype and the exemplar units are unsuitable in detail, but want to comprehend which of these two models furnish a greater explanation of how it categorize objects.

To empirically experiment competing models, researchers attempt to design experimental stipulations that lead to reverse qualitative or ordinal predictions from the two models. These qualitative checks are designed to be parameter free, i.e., the models are compelled to make these predictions for any value of the free parameters.

Even supposing it is feasible to construct qualitative tests, it is also informative to evaluate the quantitative accuracy too. The last step is typically to start all over and reformulate the theoretical framework and construct new models in light of the suggestions got from new experimental results. Model progress and testing is an under-no-circumstances-ending process. New experimental findings are learned at all times, posing new challenges to previous models. Prior items have to be modified or improved to account for these new outcomes, or in some cases, we have to discard the old models and start all over. For this reason, the modeling procedure produces an evolution of models that develop and become more powerful over time as the Science in a field develops.

2.4. Impacts of Knowledge Domain Modeling in Cognitive Systems

2.4.1. Multiple Levels of Computational Cognitive Modeling

A strategic decision that one has to make with respect to Cognitive Science is the level(s) of analysis (i.e., level(s) of abstraction) at which one models cognitive agents. Computational cognitive modeling can vary in terms of level of process details and granularity of input and output, and as a result is also carried out in a multitude of phases. The problem of multiple phases of computational cognitive modeling, drawing upon the work of Sun, Coward, and Zenzen. We must be aware that ordinary theories of multi-degree evaluation considers that there are quite a lot of stages, each of which involves one more quantity of computationally important point.

In the recent work in Theoretical Foundations of Cognitive Science, it has become commonplace to separate three distinct levels of analysis of information-processing systems. David Courtnay Marr, a British Neuroscientist and Physiologist has introduced the three levels the computational, the algorithmic, and the implementation levels. In Marr's concept, first, there is the computational concept stage, where one has to verify the right computation to be performed, its objectives, and the logic of the strategies in which the computation is to be done.

Second, there is the representation and algorithm level, where one has to be concerned with accomplishing the computational theory decided at the first stage and, especially, the representation of the input and the output and the algorithm for the transformation from the input to the output. The third level is the hardware implementation level, in which one is supposed to physically realise the representation and algorithms decided in the second level. In step with Marr, these three stages are loosely combined; that is, they are comparatively independent.

For this reason, there is most likely a wide array of choices at each stage, independent of the other two. Some phenomena may be explained at just one or two stages. Marr emphasised the "critical" importance of formulation on the stage of computational theory, that is, the extent at which the goals and functions of a cognitive method are specific, and the internal and external constraints that make the method viable are worked out and related to each other and to the goals of computation. His motive was that the type of computation depended more on thecomputationalissuestobesolvedthanonthewaythesolutionshadtobeimplemented.

In his own phrase, "An algorithm is more likely to be understood extra conveniently by means of working out the character of the problem being solved than by way of examining the mechanism where it is embodied." Therefore, he favored a top-down procedure from an extra summary degree to a extra unique level. It mainly appears that Marr's idea focused on a large amount on the moderately-minor variations in computational abstractions. It also appears that his idea represented an over-simplification of biological reality and as a result represented an over-rationalization of cognition.

Table 1: Multiple Levels of Computational Cognitive Modeling

Level	Object of Analysis
1	Computation
2	Algorithms
3	Implementations

Table 2: Multiple Levels of Computational Cognitive Modeling

Level	Object of Analysis	Type of Analysis	Computational Model
1	Inter-agent processes	Social / Cultural	Collections of agents
2	Agents	Psychological	Individual Agents
3	Intra-agent Processes	Componential	Modular Construction of agents
4	Substrates	Physiological	Biological Realization of Modules

Another variant is Newell and Simon's three-level theory. Allen Newell was a researcher in Cognitive Psychology and Computer Science and Herbert Alexander Simon was an American Political Scientist, Economist, Sociologist, Psychologist, And Computer Scientist whose research Ranged across the fields of Cognitive Science, Cognitive Psychology, Philosophy Of Science, Economics, Public Administration, Management, Computer Science, Sociology and Political Science, unified by studies of decision-making. Newell and Simon proposed the following three levels:

1. The knowledge level, in which, why cognitive agents do certain things is explained by appealing to their goals and their knowledge, and by showing rational connections between them.
2. The symbol level, in which the knowledge and goals are encoded by symbolic structures, and the manipulation of these structures implement their connection.
3. The physical level, in which the symbol structures and their manipulations are realized in some physical form. Sometimes this three-level organization was referred to as "the classical cognitive architecture." The point being emphasized here was very close to Marr's view:

What is important is the analysis at the knowledge level and then at the symbol level, that is, identifying the task and designing symbol structures and symbol manipulation procedures suitable for it. Once this analysis is worked out, the analysis can be implemented in any available physical means. In contrast, according to Sun, Coward, and Zenzen, the differences amongst "computation," algorithms, applications, and hardware realizations, and their variants, as have been the point of interest in Marr's and Newell's and Simon's level theories, are relatively in significant.

This is due to the fact that, to begin with, the differences amongst them are frequently small, fuzzy, and refined, compared to the differences among the strategies to be modeled. Second, these extraordinary computational constructs are in reality closely tangled: One cannot specify algorithms without few considerations of possible implementations, and what is to be considered "computation" depends on algorithms, primarily the notion of algorithmic complexity, and so on. Therefore, one quite often has to take into account computation, algorithms, and implementation together somehow. Third, in keeping with Sun, Coward, and Zenzen, the separation of these computational details failed to produce any key valuable insights with regard to cognition, but theoretical baggage. Reorientation towards a systematic examination of phenomena, as a substitute of tools one utilizes for modeling them, is as a result a step in the proper path.

The standpoint of Sun, Coward, and Zenzen centered attention on the very phenomena to be studied, on their scopes, scales, degrees of abstractness, and so forth. For that reason, the differences among phases of evaluation can be roughly cast as the differences amongst disciplines, from essentially the most macroscopic to the most microscopic. These phases of evaluation incorporate the sociological phase, the psychological phase, the componential phase, and the physiological phase.

Distinct phases of modeling may be established in specified correspondence with exceptional phases of evaluation. First of all, there is the sociological level, which includes the collective habits of retailers, inter-agent techniques, socio cultural approaches, as well the interaction between marketers and their environments. It is only lately that the subject of Cognitive Science has come to adhere to the fact that cognition is, at the least partially, a social/cultural approach. To ignore the socio cultural process is to ignore a fundamental underlying determinant of individual cognition. The lack of knowledge of sociological methods could result in the lack of information of some primary constructions and constraints in cognition. For this reason, any understanding of individual cognition can be partial and incomplete when socio cultural strategies are disregarded or downplayed.

The subsequent level is the psychological level, which covers individual behaviors, beliefs, competencies, concepts, and skills. In terms of the sociological level, you can actually examine the relationship of a person's beliefs, abilities, ideas, skills and concept with those of the society and the custom, and the methods of change of these beliefs, standards, knowledge, skills and concept independent of or with regards to those of the society and the custom. At this level, you can compare human behavioral data, and evaluate them with models and with insights from the sociological level and further details from the lower levels. The third level is the componential level. It is most important to notice that in computational cognitive modeling, the computational approach of an agent is more commonly unique in phrases of accessories of the agent, i.e., in phrases of intra-agent tactics. Hence, at this level, one may just specify a cognitive structure and accessories therein. Within the procedure of analysis, one specifies vital computational methods of each component, as well as, vital connections among various components. Hence, analysis of capability and analysis of components become equal at this level. Nonetheless, at this level, unlike at the psychological level, work is more in the course of structural analysis than functional analysis. At this level, one models cognitive agents in relation to components with the theoretical language of a detailed paradigm, for example, connectionist networks or symbolic computation, or their combinations. One attributes a computational procedure to a cognitive function.

Strategies and information from the psychological level, i.e., the psychological constraints from above, which bear on the division of components and possible implementations of components, are the foremost considerations. This level may also contain biological/

physiological observations concerning plausible divisions and their implementations; that is, it could possibly incorporate suggestions from the subsequent level down the physiological level, which provides the biological restrictions. This level results in cognitive mechanisms, despite the fact that they are by and large abstract and computational, and for that reason precise, compared with physiological-level standards of details. Although this level is just about in phrases of intra-agent techniques, computational items developed therein can also be used to model processes at higher phases, including the interaction at a sociological level where multiple members are involved. This can also be comprehensive, for example, by examining interactions of more than one copy of individual agents. The lowest level of evaluation is the physiological level, that is, the biological substrate, or biological implementation of computation. This level is the focus of a range of disciplines together with Physiology, Biology, Computational Neuroscience, Cognitive Neuroscience, and so on.

Although biological substrates are not among our essential concerns right here, they will nonetheless provide valuable input as to what sort of computation is probably going to be employed and what a believable architecture must be like. The main function of this level is to facilitate evaluation at greater phases, that is, to make use of low-phases information to narrow down, at larger phases, choices in implementing componential computation and choices in selecting computational architectures.

Although computational cognitive modeling is commonly restricted to inside a detailed level at a time, this need not always be the case: Cross-level analysis and modeling can be intellectually highly enlightening, and may be essential to the progress of computational cognitive modeling in the future.

These levels described above do interact with each other and may not be easily isolated and tackled alone. Moreover, their respective areas are often combined, without specific boundaries.

2.4.2. Cognitive Processing

Cognitive processes are unobservable mental actions used to manipulate information. Cognitive processes produce cognitive products and it may be processed again, or they may be manifested in performance. For example, a student may rehearse the spelling of an irregular word over and over to learn to spell it on correctly spell it correctly on a test.

Cognitive processing can be applied to any kind of information. Students' cognitive systems have the potential to process not only various kinds of information found in educational curricula, but also information that teachers provide to students to help them achieve the educational objectives. Cognition is both an effect caused by previous events, including cognitive ones, and a cause of future events. Research on students' cognitive processing during teaching has been done mostly by learning from the text.

Students' cognitive processing during teaching consists of reciprocal interactions among their cognitive processing systems on one hand, and the curriculum and instructional cues on the other. If students were exposed to curricular information sans instructional cues, that is, without instruction, they surely would learn something.

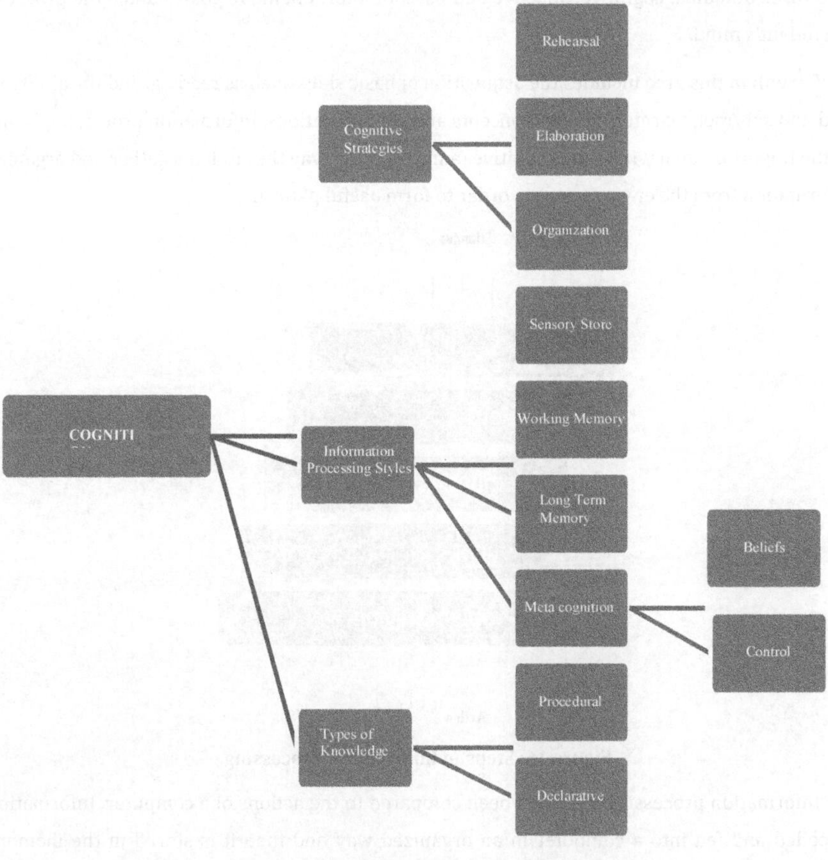

Figure 15: Cognition and its Subdivisions

The intent of supplementing curriculum with teaching is to improve the quality of students' cognitive processing beyond their natural levels. Thus, the objective of teaching is to influence the cognitive processing which is used for the students to learn.

2.4.3. Information Processing Styles

Remembrance of long-term memory is made from a large number of plans, concepts, ideas and facts against which incoming know-how is, in comparison, coded and stored. Coding incoming information depends upon choosing and defining characteristics, after which, scrutinizing similarities and differences. Nathan Kogan, an American Psychologist, and distinguished different styles of conceptualization by means of displaying to children photographs of familiar objects that had to be put into groups. Educational goals are divided into three domains: cognitive, affective and psychomotor. Cognitive goals handle the progress of student's mind.

Growth in this area includes the acquisition of basic skills such as reading, and the ability to add and subtract, learning of facts, concepts and generalizations. Information processing is one of the important goal within the cognitive family. It is the way the students gather and organize information from the environment in order to form useful pattern.

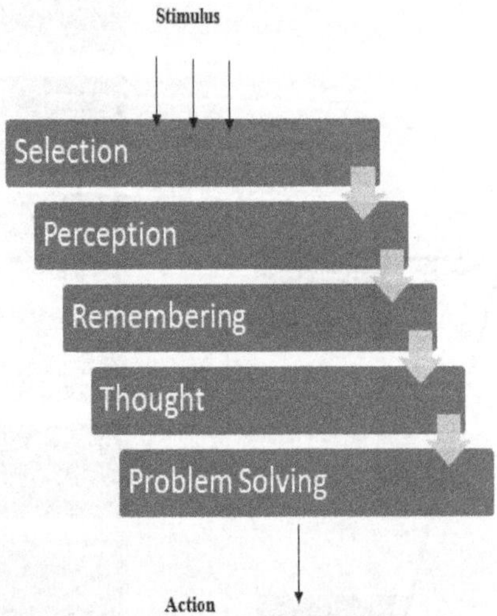

Figure 16: Steps in Information Processing

Information processing has often been compared to the actions of a computer. Information is coded and fed into a computer in an organized way and then it is stored in the memory banks. When any of that information is required the computer is asked to produce it. The machine searches for the relevant information and reproduces or prints out the items requested.

2.4.4. *Information Processing Models*

Information processing models are teaching strategies based on information processing theory that are designed to help students to learn content, at the same time, as they practice thinking skills under the guidance and direction of an active teacher. In recent years considerable emphasis has been placed on the school's role in the development of students' thinking skills. (Link, 1985; Costa, 1985). Educators are recognizing that this no longer sufficient to simply teach the students what they should know, but in addition, they must be taught how to know. Information processing specifically provides one valuable framework for addressing the development of students' thinking skills and abilities.

2.4.5. *Cognitive Models as Users*

Cognitive models simulations of human behavior now perform tasks, ranging in complexity, from simple mental arithmetic to controlling simulations of complex real-time computer-based systems, such as nuclear power plants. In the future these models will become even more powerful and useful. Providing cognitive models access to users' tasks can be done in three ways. In the first, the task simulation is implemented in the cognitive modeling language. This is the best approach when the focus of the modeling is mainly on the internal cognitive aspects and when the task is quite simple. Numerous models have used this approach, (Newell and Simon, Peck and John, and Ritter et al). In the second method, a simulation of the user's taskis implemented in a simulation language, but the interface or task cannot be directly used by human users, and the model's task simulation might not provide a visible representation of the task or of the model's behavior.

The early versions of Embedded Parallel Instruction Computing (EPIC), for example, used this approach, as do numerous other models. In the third method, the task simulation can be operated by both the user and the model.

This approach is superior when the simulation already exists, or when modeling complex dynamic domains where the task is too difficult to simulate using the previous approaches. It is preferable for the model to use the existing interface because fewer assumptions have to be made about equivalencies of the interfaces, and less work is required, because only one interface is created. We describe here an approach for allowing cognitive models more direct access to the interface supers perceive.

This is done by adapting ideas taken from User Iinterface Management Systems (UIMSes) and extending them in a principled way, so that cognitive models can interact with any interface built within the UIMS.

This will allow cognitive models to be utilized as an interface design and evaluation tool on a wider range of interactive systems as previously envisioned. We next present the advantages of this approach for HCI and for modeling.

2.4.6. The Advantages for HCI

Cognitive models have been efficiently utilized in three main methods by using Human- PCI interplay (HCI). The first method is to help evaluate the effectiveness of special designs with the help of cognitive models to predict task performance times. The Model Human Processor, the Keystroke Level Model, and particularly the GOMS family of techniques have all been successfully deployed in the laboratory and in the industry. These models can support, create and choose higher designs, in many instances saving thousands of dollars. The next step for this approach is to provide and incorporate these and extra complex models in design tools to provide feedback for designers.

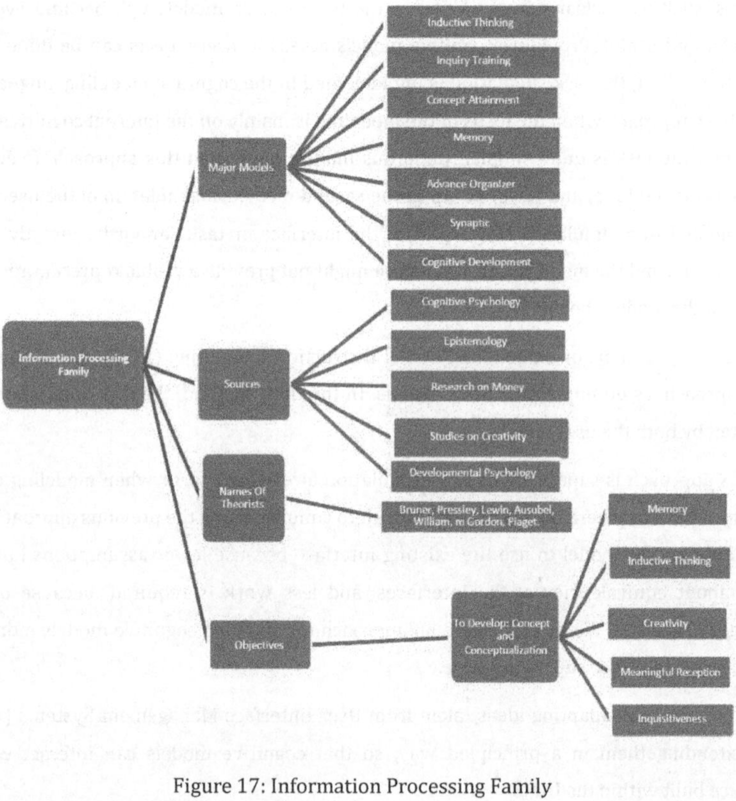

Figure 17: Information Processing Family

The second method is utilizing cognitive units to provide help, such as with an embedded assistant. In short, models can be utilized to modify interaction to support users with their tasks. This procedure has been employed in cognitive tutors.

A few of these model-based tutors may also be regarded as an example of what are probably described as embedded agents or embedded intelligent assistants. Your next step forward is to make the progress of such models an extra actions methods. The third way is by way of making use of models as an alternative for users. These models are useful for populating synthetic environments, for example, to simulate fighter aircraft crews in a simulated war scenario.

In the future they will also lead to models that can test interfaces by behaving like a user. The next step for this approach is to provide models with more realistic inputs and outputs mirroring human performance and to apply them more widely. Using models as users has been envisioned before, but has not yet been widely applied.

One major impediment to each of these uses of cognitive modeling in HCI has been the difficulty of connecting the cognitive models to their task environment; either the connection or the interface has to be built, sometimes both. There is an additional requirement that the connection should mimic the limitations and capabilities of human performance.

2.5. Cognition and Programming

2.5.1. The Relationship between Cognition and Programming

The fields of cognition and programming are related in three main methods. First, Cognitive Psychology is situated on a 'computational metaphor,' in which the human intellect is obvious as a style of information processor much like a PC. Secondly, Cognitive Psychology offers ways for analyzing the processes underlying performance in computing tasks. Thirdly, programming a well-defined task, and there is an increasing quantity of programmers, which makes it an ultimate task in which to learn cognitive procedures in a real-world domain.

2.5.2. The Computational Metaphor

Cognitive psychology is the study of the mechanisms in which mental approaches are carried out, and the kinds of knowledge required for each and every approach. Cognitive techniques incorporate perception, attention, language creation, memory storage and retrieval, problem-solving, understanding and reasoning. These are all operations performed on information by a Central Processing Unit (CPU) with associated memory, to produce an appropriate output. Like a computer, information flows through phases of cognitive processing and storage to give a response output. Also like a computer, information is represented in symbolic form. Recent theories of information processing retain the concept of information in the form of symbols being stored and operated upon before output of a response, although their components are more interactive and less stage dependent than those of earlier theories.

Zenon Walter Pylyshyn, a Cognitive Scientist and Philosopher, argues that since both human and computer output results from operations carried out on symbols, cognition is literally a kind of computation. A computer system can be described at three levels -- the software, features of the implementation of programs on the hardware, and the hardware itself. Software, implementation, and hardware can be used to describe a cognitive system. The cognitive software consists of mental procedures and knowledge representations used in performing cognitive tasks. For example, strategies such as means-ends analysis are equivalent to programs for undertaking certain problem solving tasks. The 'cognitive implementation' of software concerns the mechanisms for carrying out procedures and knowledge representation, such as symbol manipulation, storage, retrieval and so on. For example, limitations of attention and memory constrain the knowledge and procedures available during problem solving. Studying cognitive implementation despite identifying constraints on cognitive performance, is both more difficult and consistent with research into programming that is mainly concerned with identifying the knowledge and mental procedures used in programming.

The 'cognitive hardware' consists of the physiological structures, notably the brain upon which cognitive processes are implemented. Physiological structures are not a central concern of Cognitive Psychology, since one of the major assumptions underlying the computational metaphor is that cognitive processes are determined by their function, and not by the structure of the hardware upon which they are based. The computational metaphor dominates Cognitive Psychology, although some argue that accounting for cognition in terms of symbol manipulation is implausible, and that the biological basis of cognition should not be ignored.

A recent development, which offers an alternative to the computational metaphor for studying cognition is 'connection.' Connectionist modelling is closer to the level of cognitive hardware, in that it uses the parallel processing capabilities of the brain to explain how cognitive processes are carried out. Connectionist models are not of direct relevance to programming research because they focus on cognitive hardware rather than software. However, future developments in parallel computer architectures may include concepts such as constraint satisfaction programming. The cognitive skills necessary to cope with programming a parallel processing machine may, therefore, be an important topic for future research.

2.5.3. *Important Themes in Cognition*

A division is often made between knowledge. At the level of cognitive implementation, theories of representation describe the form in which individual units of knowledge are stored. Pylyshyn claims that all information is represented as propositions, which are language-like assertions retaining only the meaning of individual items of knowledge, rather than representing only the meaning of individual items of a perceptual input. Alternating, Paivio's dual code theory suggests that verbal information is represented in spatial image or analogue form, Analogue representations may determine performance in some programming tasks. For example, Julianne Ormerod, Assistant with MIT Department of Brain and Cognitive Sciences, found that different reasoning strategies are used in comprehending diagrammatic and list representations of prolog clauses. More important to programming research however is the organization of knowledge at the level of cognitive software, for example, the schema and strategy accounts of programming.

2.5.4. *Schema Representations*

An important approach to describing representation at a cognitive software level is the schema. A schema consists of a set of propositions that are organized by their semantic content. A perceptual input, cognitive goal or output of a cognitive process may evokea schema with a related semantic content.

Once evoked, it provides an organized body of knowledge which is appropriate for the task in hand. For example, Figure 1 shows a schematic representation of part of the knowledge a programmer may possess about programming languages. If a programmer is required to think of an alternative to iteration for dealing with lists, the words 'iteration' and 'lists' will activate the schema 'programming languages.'

This will allow the programmer to access knowledge about looping constructs, and thus generate alternatives such as 'recursion.' There are two basic principles of schema theories; first, that cognitive processing is guided and limited by the application of prior knowledge and secondly, that schemas contain relatively abstract knowledge which is independent of any one event.

Thus, a schema highlights relevant information in a task domain, and may add new information when there is insufficient information in a task domain. Figure 17 illustrates a number of components of schema, such as hierarchical organization, default values for generating information which is not present in the task domain, and slots which can be filled by matching information from the task domain.

A schema offers a method for limiting the amount of inputed information, or 'bottom-up' control, that is needed to perform a task. Schema provides a 'top-down' control, using prior knowledge to restrict the operations that may be under taken.

In Figure 18, the schema 'programming language' represents part of the general knowledge a person may have about programming languages. This schema is linked to others. The particular episode represents an encounter with a previously unknown language. The shaded areas represent information available for a particular task. Information may originate from the task domain as 'fillers' for the schema slots, or from the schema as 'default values' where no conflicting task domain information is present. This representation is also a schematic representation.

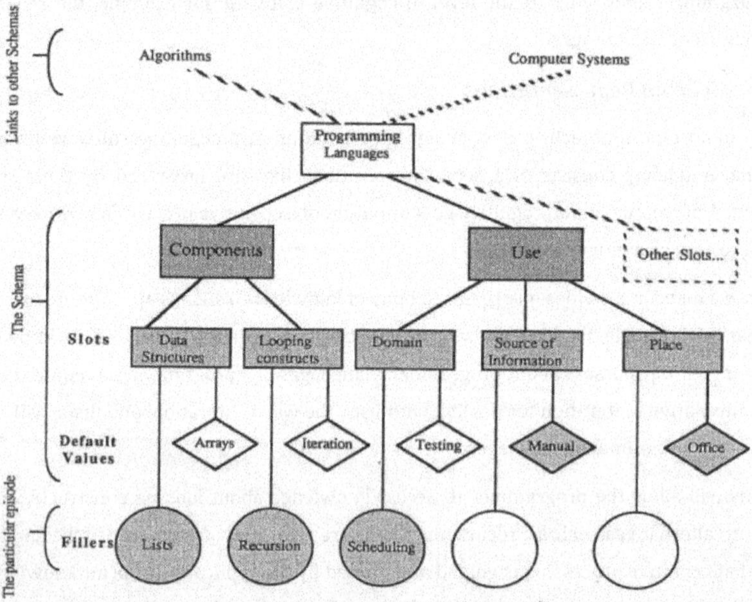

Figure 18: Schema Representations

2.6. Structure of Cognitive Computing Applications

2.6.1. Psycholinguistics and Programming Research

The review has, for reasons of space, been highly selective. The most obvious omission is a discussion of psycholinguistics.

In part this is because many important concepts are covered in other topics, which illustrates how cognitive processes cannot be neatly partitioned as they were in early cognitive models.

Thus the focus of research into programming is not on syntactic features of different languages, but on semantic programming knowledge. However, as in recent theories of language understanding, the interaction between semantic and syntactic components of the programming task has recently been highlighted.

2.6.2. Quantum Structures in Cognitive and Social Science

A primary concern in cognitive and Social Science concerns the identification of the principles guiding human cognitive acts such as categorization, decision-making and behavior under uncertainty.

Identifying these mechanisms would have manifold implications for fields ranging from Psychology to Economics, Finance, Politics, Computer Science, and AI. The predominant theoretical paradigm rests on a classical conception of probability and logic theory.

According to this paradigm, humans make choices with the aid of following the foundations of Boole's logic - named after the nineteenth century mathematician George Boole, Boolean logic is a form of algebra in which all values are reduced to either TRUE or FALSE. While the probabilistic aspects of these decisions can be formalized through Kolmogorov's probability theory, named after Andrey Nikolaevich Kolmogorov, a Russian mathematician, probability theory is that part of mathematics that aims to provide insight into the phenomena that depend on chance or on uncertainty.

This classical approach was believed to provide a quite complete and accurate account of human decision-making at both a normative level (describing what people should do) and a descriptive level (describing what people actually do).

However, starting from the seventies, experimental studies of human judgment, conceptual categorization, human perception, and behavioral economics have shown that this classical conception is basically problematical, i.e., the cognitive models based on these mathematical structures do not have the capacity to capture how humans make decisions in circumstances involving uncertainty.

In the last decade, an alternative scientific paradigm has arisen that employs an additional and extra general modeling scheme; it makes use of the mathematical formalism of quantum theory to model circumstances and techniques in cognitive and Social Science.

This new approach has not only met with considerable success, but is becoming increasingly accepted in the scientific community, having attracted interest from important scientists, top journals, funding institutions, and media.

Prisoners' dilemmas; violations of the Sure-Thing principle; disjunction effects; conjunction and disjunction fallacies; Allais, Ellsberg and Machina contradictions, wherein the application of the quantum mechanical formalism has displayed significant efficiency over traditional modeling schemes of a classical type.

The Frontiers research subject "Quantum structures in Cognitive and Social Science" presents a summary of current study that applies the formalism of quantum concept to cognitive and socioeconomic domains.

The term "quantum" may be misleading. The intention right here is to not examine the microphysical approaches occurring in the human brain and, as an outcome, riding human judgments. Rather, it inquire into the validity of quantum conception as a normal, coherent, and a unitary paradigm for human cognition. In this respect, this study benefits from findings into the axiomatic and operational foundations of quantum physics.

The following modeling is theory-based, no longer experiment-based; that is, the models usually are not developed around a specified outcomes or test, even though they are frequently used in conjunction with empirical data to construct a stronger case.

The models are built following the general epistemological and technical constraints of quantum conception; hence, the successes of this quantum conception- established modeling suggest that it might provide a general theory for human cognition.

This Research Topic Develops around three Main Directions of Research, as Follows

1. The deep causes underlying the success of the quantum paradigm in cognitive and socio-monetary domains are investigated.
2. Further empirical situations are identified in these domains where the quantum formalism shows advantages with respect to traditional modeling schemes, and new genuine quantum structures appear.
3. The appliance of this quantum paradigm is accelerated to the innovative and barely explored domains.

The first set of results relate to conceptual categorization and knowledge representation. Researchers scrutinized the results of a cognitive test on conjunctions and negations of natural concepts, exhibiting that a quantum-theoretic probabilistic model in Hilbert space truly denotes the collected data, at variance with a set-theoretic Kolmogorovian model. This outcome is elucidated by assuming the existence of two kinds of reasoning in human cognition, a dominant emergent reasoning, and a secondary logical reasoning. A few mathematical features of this quantum-theoretic model on conceptual conjunctions and negations are developed through the introduction of unitary operators in Hilbert space. The quantum-theoretic approach can be inferred as a suitable generalization of the Rosch's prototype theory, wherein prototypes are context-dependent and may interfere when concepts combine.

The second set of results relate to the modeling of human decision-making. Research discovers an alternative quantum-theoretic approach, the quantum-like Bayesian network, to define the paradoxes associated with the violation of the Sure-Thing Principle (It is a decision making standard that proposes there is no need to consider uncertainty in a decision, which would not impact the decision anyway) in experiments on human judgments. Their model is in a good agreement with different sets of empirical data. Opinion papers evaluate some current progress on the quantum similarity model in Hilbert space which rightly represents human similarity judgments. Decision-making errors and preference reversal are also examined within their quantum decision theory. Studies examine the concept of complementarily in human cognition, and assert that the way in which it is used in quantum physics can also be useful in Cognitive Science. Human perception is the object of the study where a quantum model is developed of the sensation-perception dynamics, exemplifying it by means of the model of bi-stable (an electronic circuit which has two stable states) perception of a specific ambiguous figure, the Schröder stair (It is an optical illusion which is a two-dimensional drawingwhichmaybeperceivedeitherasadrawingofastaircaseleadingfromlefttorightdownwards or the same staircase only turned upside down; a classical example of perspective reversal in psychology of perception. It is named after the German natural scientist Heinrich G.F. Schröder).

Finally, studies identify a significant violation of temporal Bell inequalities in a set of cognitive tests.

The violation indicates, according to the authors, the presence of temporal entanglement between binary human performances on unconscious choices at a given time and binary random outcomes at a different time. In all these approaches, the presence of quantum structures in cognition is determined by the fact that the cognitive systems under investigation share a common feature, namely contextually.

A different position with respect to the presence of contextually in cognition is assumed, where to apply a theory of (non) contextually to analyze Series-Parallel (SP) mental architectures.

The third set of results concern advanced applications of the quantum-mathematical formalism to wider ranges of social science. Researchers propose an inverse Potts model, typically used in statistical quantum field theory, to reconstruct the node states in a real-world social network.

Haven explored the properties of two types of potential functions, inspired by classical and quantum physics that can be potentially employed to model financial information, including preferences towards risk and uncertainty.

Finally, studies investigate different, but mutually related, aspects of parallelism within the framework of quantum computation, cognition and music, and study potential applications of quantum computational semantics in both natural and musical language.

Leaving aside the specific differences between the approaches above, most of them agree in claiming that quantum structures are systematically present in cognitive and Social Science phenomena, and that quantum-inspired models are more efficient than traditional set-theoretic models of probability.

Is Hilbert space really the place where all these phenomena can be modeled? Is "quantum" the end of the story? Is there any empirical deviation from quantum predictions? We do not have yet an answer to these questions.

This is why we believe that the road that will lead further to possibly a generally accepted quantum theory of human decision-making will still be full of fascinating surprises.

2.6.3. Creating a Semantic (Linguistic) Vocabulary

In the previous examples, we examined the nature of fuzzy sets and mapped a single fuzzy set over the domain of project durations. This fuzzy set defined our idea of what we mean by a "long project."

In most real-world cases, we do not associate an event field with a single fuzzy set, but we disintegrate the event field into a collection of overlapping fuzzy sets that define the over-all semantics of the data. Figure 19 illustrates how the event field duration is disintegrated into three fuzzy sets.

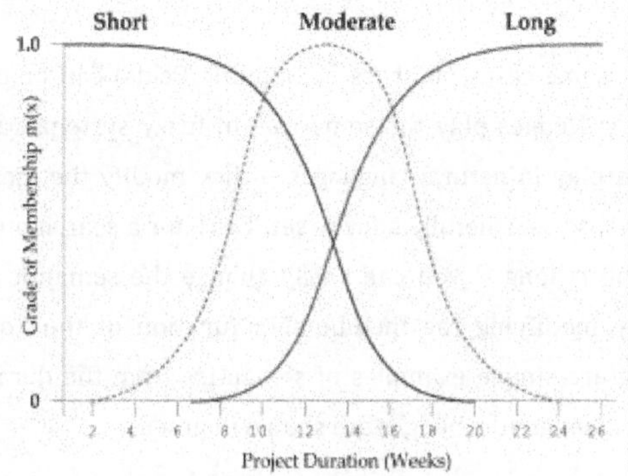

Figure 19: Creating a Semantic (Linguistic) Vocabulary

These three fuzzy sets define the vocabulary for accessing the contents of the duration event field. They provide a linguistic framework based on the names and the inherent semantics of the member fuzzy sets. The fuzzy set semantics do not comprise an unique partitioning of the data.

A Linguistic Variable

A collection of fuzzy sets defining the semantics of an event field is, by convention, called a Fuzzy Term Set (that is, a set of fuzzy terms). The Term Set is the means by which an event field (or a calculated field) is converted to a Linguistic Variable. A linguistic variable maps data to a set of overlapping fuzzy sets which describe the semantics of the data.

This transformation is based on the way information is now retrieved from the field: we use the names of the fuzzy sets (in a fuzzy proposition or expression) instead of the underlying values of the data. Thus, instead of,

Where Duration > 10

We use a linguistically based search process that is based on the names of the underlying fuzzy sets.

Where Duration is Long

Such a request does not filter and produce a collection of events. Instead, the result is an collection of events containing the degree to which they match (are compatible with) the semantic concept "Long." This is the Compatibility Index. The idea of compatibility with one or more features of the Linguistic Variable is the foundation on which the search's cognitive model is constructed.

2.6.4. Hedges

A fuzzy set (and in some cases numbers or numeric fields) can be changed by linguistic modifiers called hedges. Hedges play the same role in fuzzy systems (as well as search) as adverbs and adjectives play in natural languages -- they modify the meaning of an attached term. The term, in this case, is generally a fuzzy set. Thus, for a search on the project duration field -- project duration is long -- you can easily change the semantic intentionality of the search by dynamically modifying the membership function of the Long fuzzy set. As an example, the following are simple examples of semantics from the duration event field that have been modified by a hedge (the hedges are shown in green),

- Duration is not long.
- Duration is very long.
- Duration is very very long.
- Project duration is somewhat long.
- Duration is not very long.
- Duration is slightly long.
- Duration is around moderate and above moderate.
- Duration is somewhat not very much above moderate.

A hedge is designed to change fuzzy sets in a way that reflects the ordinary meaning of the linguistic transformation.

Thus, the hedge, when applied to a fuzzy set, changes the shape of the membership function so that, for linear, growth, and declining curves, only values toward the right of the curve gave high membership values. For bell shaped curves, the membership values around the central value are elevated. The effect is, for any membership value, to select only those data values that have the ordinary meaning of "very high." Such changes in the semantic nature of the fuzzy set are invisible to the user and only reflected in the composition of the events that are returned by the search.

Hedges change the shape of fuzzy sets (and can also create fuzzy sets from event field values or numeric constants) by changing the membership function according to rules that reflect the perceived psychology of the hedge's use in ordinary language. These changes are, in many cases, implemented as rather complex behavior-oriented algorithms. There are six classes of hedges.

Examples of the hedge modifications are provided for four hedges commonly used in both Conceptual Search and the Conceptual Rule System.

2.7. Summary

- In this chapter we briefly discussed about Cognitive model can be used to simulate or predict human behavior or performance, problem solving and mental task processes in a computerized model.
- The domain model is a representation of meaningful real-world concepts, concepts include the data involved in the business and rules the business uses in relation to that data.
- Cognitive programming as the paradigm for this user-machine interaction, whereby the machine is no longer viewed as a tool at the disposal of the user.
- Applications based on Watson are being developed for both the vertical and the horizontal markets.

The difference between the Cognitive computing and data analytics are discussed in the upcoming chapters.

CHAPTER 3

Cognitive Computing VS Data Analytics

3.1. Introduction

The aim of cognitive computing is to simulate human idea strategies in a computerized version. With the use of self-mastering algorithms that uses facts like mining, pattern reputation and natural language processing, the computer can mimic the manner the human mind works.

While computers were faster at calculations and processing than human beings for decades, they have not been capable to accomplish obligations that humans take for granted as simple as understanding natural language or recognizing unique objects in an image.

Figure 20: Cognitive Computing

Source:http://www.businesscloudnews.com/files/2016/01/AI-Artificial-Intelligence-Machine-Learning-Cognitive-Computing-2.jpg.

A few individuals say that Cognitive Computing represents the one-third technology of computing: We have moved from computers that tabulate sums to programmable systems and now to cognitive systems.

Those cognitive systems, maximum notably IBM's Watson, rely upon deep gaining knowledge of algorithms and neural networks to process statistics by comparing it to a learning set of facts. The bigger data the device is exposed to, the more it learns and the extra accurate it will become through the years, and the neural community is a complex "tree" of decisions the computer can make to arrive at an answer.

3.2. Why Cognitive Analytics?

A cognitive device can provide real-time solutions to questions posed in natural language by way of looking through large amounts of data which have been entered into its knowledge base, making the feel of context, and computing the maximum possible solution. As developers and customers "train" the system, the solutions become more reliable and increasingly treasured over the years.

For instance, a doctor can use cognitive analytics to quickly examine through scientific journals, clinician notes, patient records, and different documents to discover highly relevant information to improve a diagnosis or treatment plan. A customer care representative can rapidly answer a customer's query about camping equipment by using a cognitive system that drags information from product descriptions, customer reviews, sales histories, topical blogs, and travel magazines.

Many organizations may choose to preserve and develop their superior analytics capabilities at the same time as a cognitive technology continues to develop; however, for groups that wants to discover real-time answers hidden within big amounts of numerous data's.

3.3. The Benefits of Cognitive Analytics

Mine Untapped Data Sources

In preference to ignore bulky data, businesses can use cognitive analytics to quickly tap unstructured data, text files, images, emails, social posts, and more for valuable insights.

Provide Personalized Services

Speedy, service provider is now not sufficient to win these days' consumers. Their loyalty is won by way of groups that could provide incredibly customized delivery service primarily based on what the data says about the person's preferences and history.

Improve Service Consistency and Quality

Individuals regularly come to unique conclusions which are based totally upon the same information. Cognitive analytics can assist and reduce the subjectivity in choice-making and do it faster via tracing how choices are made and measuring the resulting outcomes, permitting key practices to be shared throughout the organization.

Enhance knowledge sharing cognitive analytics can be used to increase knowledge sharing, providing fast access to highly relevant answers and insights on demand.

3.4. What to Do Now in Cognitive Analytics?

As cognitive applications force more business processes and automate decisions, society is working for vastly inclusive legal, regulatory and policy frameworks to manage compliance, risk and implications.

Cognitive Analytics will become the Principal Personalization Tool

Cognitive systems have become challenging, context-conscious, customized interaction agents; the future of cognitive applications in our lives is pervasive personalization. Cognitive systems will definitely increase and understand the geospatial and temporal context of everything we are doing, and supply the responses which is reliable to the contexts.

Cognitive Analytics will Start to Automate Most Data Analysis

Cognitive systems are implementing untried learning to automate sensing and detection of deep patterns and level in complex data sets.

Machine learning is enabling automated systems to understand new concepts on their own and train themselves to be used.

Cognitive Analytics will Drive Further Scaling in Cloud Data Services

Cognitive systems are scaling inexorably and indefinitely. As cognition as a service offering, such as IBM Watson increase implementation, the scalability will expand within the volume, velocity and variety of data and algorithms begin executing, as well as, the resource requirements.

Begin with the End in Mind

Leaders who stand to gain more value from analytics could start by imagining how people access and use information to improve decisions and deliver more consistently high-quality, personalized products and services.

Build the Business Case

Examine labor-intensive procedures consisting of criminal studies or customer support that would be streamlined by deploying cognitive technologies. Determine if the capability cost-savings could fund the capabilities needed.

Start Small

In case your company should benefit from Cognitive Analytics, start with a pilot project to benefit experience and enhance your commercial enterprise use case.

3.5. How Does Cognitive Computing Relate to Analytics?

Before answering, let us outline what we speak approximately. In step with INFORMS, Analytics is the clinical technique of transforming data into perception for making better decisions. According to Wikipedia, Cognitive Computing combines AI and machine-mastering algorithms, in a technique which tries to rear the conduct of the human brain. An example is provided by using the IBM agency's Watson machine.

One should dispute these definitions; however they are true enough to make sure we understand the question effectively. A primary set of solutions to that query declare that Cognitive Computing is nothing, but any other analytic level sitting on top of the present ones. We have seen many variations of it; however, the larger one is depicted below. It is far satisfactory of what we have seen due to the fact its axis have some advantages that is worth. Specially, it is far real that one of the promises of Cognitive Computing is to provide a new user experience that leverages communication in natural language. Its learning capabilities are also very appealing and intuitive to use.

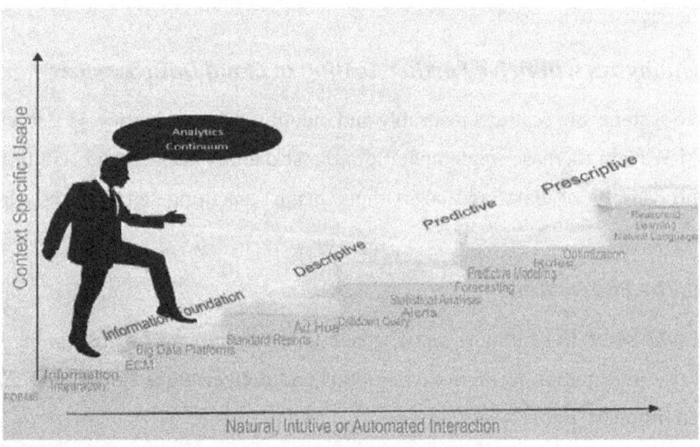

Figure 21: An Extended Analytics Ladder

3.5.1. Cognitive Computing Can be Used in each of the Existing Analytics Levels

Let's describe this in a minute, but before that we should revisit analytics and its purpose. The purpose of an analytics solution is to enable business decisions based on data. It does not necessarily mean that such solutions must compute decisions. It means that whatever their output, they must support decision making. In short, analytics are a journey from data to decisions and actions, via the use of many different techniques and tools.

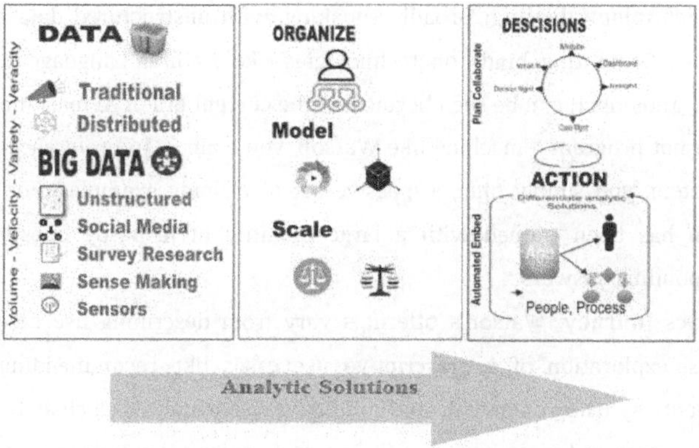

Figure 22: The Purpose of Analytics

As discussed in The Analytics Maturity Model, we can distinguish several analytic levels. In some cases we just provide ways to view and explore the data as is. This is called descriptive analytics.

In some different instances, we provide insights (egg styles or relationships) located inside the data, via data analysis for example. That is known as diagnostic analytics. In yet other instances, we can use these insights to make a few predictions, for example, forecasting future income levels, or figuring out which employee is most likely to leave, that is known as predictive analytics. Closing, in some instances, we are able to compute choices, for example, plan production to achieve forecast sales; this is known as prescriptive analytics. These one-of-a-kind stages depend totally on what is automatic and what is left to individuals before decisions can be made; if we examine analytics in this manner, then where would Cognitive Computing fit? Would it not cross past prescriptive analytics on some distance, right? of course not! So, where it fits?, and the way it fits, is that different from analytics?

It is quite simple actually: Cognitive Computing extends analytic levels to a new kind of data, using new technologies. Let us look at each of these:

- **Data**: In a nutshell, Cognitive Computing is especially useful when data is a large corpus of free text documents. Think of Wikipedia, which became the data used for "Jeopardy" by IBM Watson. Jeopardy is an American television quiz show where contestants are supplied with answers and they need to form questions. Consider the scientific literature used in Watson for Oncology. In these instances, Cognitive Computing is used to investigate millions of open-text documents to support an extensive range of activities.

- **New technology dealing**: Broadly speaking, with unstructured data and open text, Cognitive Computing binds on technologies like Natural Language Processing and system studying. It can be seen because of the current era of AI machines. Particularly, you do not program a machine like Watson, you train it. In preference to coding into the system, you simply offer a massive set of training examples. For instance, IBM Watson has been trained with a large quantity of Jeopardy questions and their corresponding answers.
- **Analytics Journey**: Watson's offerings vary from describing use cases inclusive of records, exploration of a prescriptive use cases like recommending most cancer treatments by using diagnostic and predictive use instances, such as finding relations between ideas and ideas buried in literature. Cognitive Computing instead extends the analytics adventure to areas that have been unapproachable with more traditional analytics strategies like enterprise intelligence, records, and operations studies. Moreover, traditional analytics and cognitive computing are not at the same time distinct. As an example, Watson Analytics leverages Cognitive Computing to provide the advantage of traditional analytic strategies without their complexity.

3.6. Data Analytics of Cognitive Computing

Astronomical centers, including the brand new era of radiotele scopes, e.g., Low-Frequency Array (LOFAR) are frequently considered as real examples of the form of big data generators, which are unexpectedly emerging in an extensive range in various clinical fields.

Telescope facilities like LOFAR can robotically produce data sets of 100 terabyte consistent with present day, and new facilities together with the *Square Kilometer Array* (SKA), a large multi radio telescope, will generate data sets that include billions of sources. The restrained capacity to process these big data sets and familiarize the complexity of the archived data products is already rising as a prime bottleneck in the clinical exploitation of these new systems.

Astronomers are in an awesome role to benefit from the nature of their records and the acute scale of their problem -- telescopes like LOFAR and SKA make for interesting trialbeds for the improvement of novel strategies and advanced structures that may have additional value in lots of other fields, such as those with big societal gain via industrial and business application. By helping to broaden and become early adopters of these progresses, astronomers have the opportunity to make wonderful progresses in completely exploiting developments in Data Analytics and Cognitive Computing, so that it will absolutely make the most massive sets of multi-dimensional, multi-wavelength and multi-messenger data coming their way. The DOME collaboration is in particular well positioned to, in addition, develop those thoughts.

Big data is usually defined in phrases of the three V's – volume, speed and variety. All three traits apply to enormous information – the first two are apparent (big data sets and data streaming or data "in movement,") and the third "range" relates to the range of data type in astronomy. This can be taken into consideration to describe the myriad of different devices, wavelength levels/ messenger type recorder, and information layout. A fourth V, "Veracity" is vital in all areas of analytics, and is widely recognized to astronomers managing with measurements which may be usually uncertain (because of the limits of the instrumentation) or likely distorted (e.g.,due to the presence of manmade interference in radio astronomy records units).

Studying the aggregate of conventional data resources with unstructured data (for example, Social Media) is presently a huge viable initiative, and the investments being made via large commercial organizations is extensive.

A few of the developments now being made through a spread of big data initiatives are likely to be relevant to astronomy now, not only the distributed server hardware, however, also the underlying software program infrastructure, for example, scalable open-supply software along with Hadoop, facilitating disbursed processing of large data sets across clusters of commodity servers.

In order to understand and predict the behavior of customers, forecast financial tendencies, or uncover operational insights that may increase efficiency, large investments are being made in areas such as data analytics. Often, correlations and patterns in the information should be diagnosed speedily, generally in real-time, if they are to realise their absolute commercial effect. Brute pressure correlations of all information types are leading to new and sudden insights that had been not intuitively apparent from the start.

Naturally, it is vital now not to confuse correlation with causality, however, a brute pressure approach, coupled with state-of-the-art pattern popularity algorithms, can screen difficult-to-spot connections.

3.7. Big Data Analytics Adoption

Big data analytics is a fast-growing and influential practice. However, how many user organizations are actually doing it? To find out, this report's survey asked respondents: "Does your organization execute advanced analytics against big data today?"

Advanced analytics are fairly common today: Roughly three quarters (74%) of organizations surveyed have adopted some form of analytics today, regardless of the analytic method, or tool type, whether with big data or not. This reveals a strong adoption of advanced analytics, which isn't a surprise, given that it's been around for at least 15 years. (Later, Figure 23 will reveal which analytic methods are the most common today).

Analytics doesn't require big data: The two get jammed into the same sentence so much lately that we forget that they don't have to go together. In fact, 40% of survey respondent's practice advanced analytics without big data.

One-third of organizations (34%) do big data analytics today, although it's new. In other words, they practice some form of advanced analytics, and they apply it to big data. This is a respectable presence for big data analytics, given the novelty of the combination of advanced analytics and big data.

The Organization will Execute Advanced Analytics against Data Analytics Today

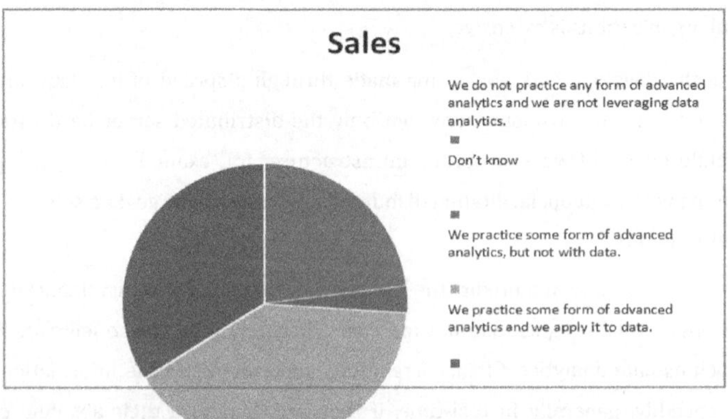

Figure 23: Analytics against Data Analytics Today

3.7.1. Benefits of Big Data Analytics

Organizations have adopted big data analytics in appreciable numbers. To determine the potential benefits that are driving the adoption, Transforming Data with Intelligence's (TDWI) survey asked: "Which of the following benefits would ensue if your organization implemented some form of big data analytics?" The most likely benefits are those most often selected by survey respondents, and the likelihood of a benefit declines as the list proceeds downward.

Inadequate staffing and skills are the leading barriers to big data analytics (46%). After all, many organizations are still new to big data analytics and its skill set is not quite the same as that for business intelligence and data warehousing, for which most organizations have developed their skills. Other skill-related barriers include the difficulty of architecting a big data analytic system (33%) and problems with making big data usable for end users (22%).

A lack of business support can hinder a big data analytics program: Survey respondents pointed to a lack of business sponsorship (38%) and a lack of a compelling business case (28%), plus the related issue of overall cost (42%).

Problems with database software can be barriers to big data analytics: Issues arise when the current database software lacks in-database analytics (32%), has scalability problems with big data (23%), can't process analytic queries fast enough (22%), or cannot load data fast enough (21%). In a related issue, managing big data in a data warehouse is challenging when that warehouse is modeled for reports and Online Analytical Processing (OLAP) only (22%). Possible barriers entered by survey respondents selecting "other" include competing with other initiatives, lack of test and control rigor, and sourcing and rationalizing big data from multiple systems.

In an organization, the top potential barriers to implementing big data analytics are listed below:

Inadequate staffing or skills for big data analytics	-	46%
Cost, overall	-	42%
Lack of business sponsorship	-	38%
The difficulty of architecting big data analytic system	-	33%
The Current database software lacks in-database analytics	-	32%
Lack of compelling business case	-	28%
Scalability problems with big data	-	23%
Cannot make big data usable for end users	-	22%
Current database software can't process analytic queries fast enough	-	22%
Current data warehouse modeled for reports and OLAP only	-	22%
Current database software cannot load data fast enough	-	21%
Can't find Hadoop experts to hire	-	11%
Can't fund Hadoop's high operational expenses	-	7%
Other	-	6%

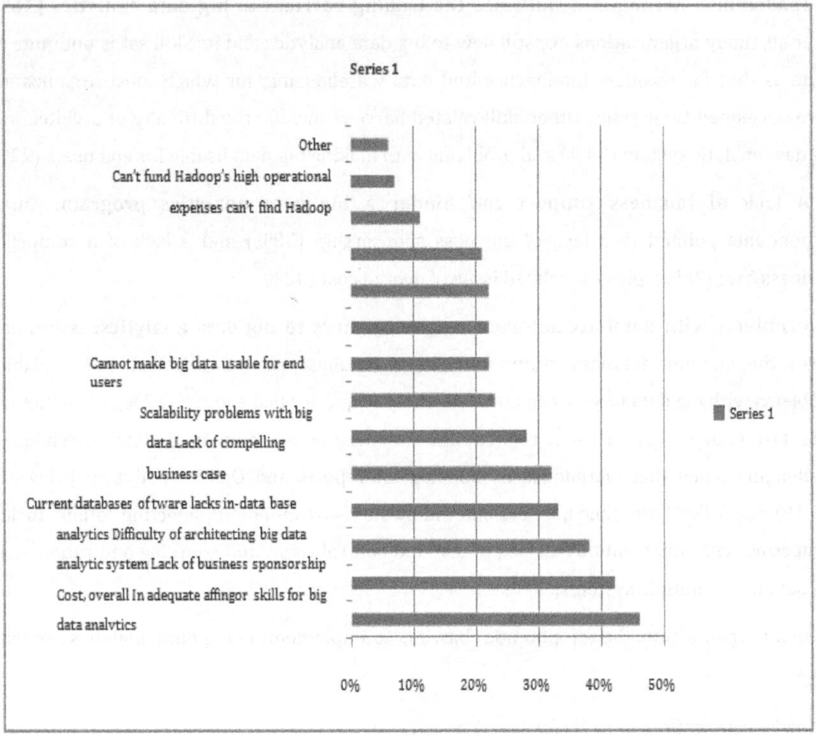

Figure 24: Top Potential Barriers to Implementing Big Data Analytics

3.7.2. What is Data Analytics What Makes it so Powerful? The Solution

Initially, It require an approach to acquire all the diverse information sources that is considerably speedier than customary "Extract, Transform and Load (ETL)." i.e., a process in data warehousing responsible for pulling data out of the source systems and placing it into a data warehouse. You need to be able to load in raw data. That implies stacking all metadata in the frame it was produced as a log record, database table, centralized computer copybook or an online networking stream. Second, you require an approach to find bits of knowledge unhampered by predefined models. You should have the capacity to emphasize with a generally utilized investigation device, for example, a spreadsheet. At last, you require an approach to picture those experiences and have those perceptions naturally refreshed. So as your business transforms, you can see and stretch out beyond those progressions.

Figure 25: Data Analytics

Source:https://www.tibco.com/blog/wpcontent/uploads/2014/01/shutterstock_147625 8831.jpg

3.7.3. Understanding the Knowledge of R Language in Data Analytics

R is an open source application bundle to participate in statistical analysis on data. R is a programming language which is utilized by data scientists, statisticians, and others who need to make a statistical analysis of information and glean key insights from knowledge utilizing mechanisms, such as regression, clustering, classification, and text evaluation. R is registered beneath GNU (normal PublicLicense).

It is developed by Ross Ihaka and Robert Gentleman at the institution of Auckland, New Zealand, which is currently handled with the aid of the R development Core workforce. It may be viewed as one more implementation of S, developed by Johan Chambers at Bell Labs. There are some major differences, however, a lot of the code written in S may also be unaltered utilizing the R interpreter engine. R provides an extensive kind of statistical, desktop studying (linear and nonlinear modeling, basic statistical exams, time-sequence analysis, classification, clustering) and graphical techniques and is mainly extensible. Rhasquitea lot of developed-in as good as improved functions for statistical, computing device studying, and visualization duties corresponding to:

- Data extraction.
- Data cleaning.
- Data loading.
- Data transformation.
- Statistical analysis.
- Predictive modelling.
- Data visualization.

It is one of the most popular open source statistical analysis applications available on the market these days. It is cross platform, has a very wide community support, and a large and ever-growing user community who are adding new packages every day. With its growing file of programs, R can now connect to exclusive facts shops, similar to MySQL, SQLite, MongoDB, and Hadoop for information storage routine.

3.7.4. Technology Foundations

Past the quandary of the mission, we must admire that each and every pattern, i.e.,massive knowledge and cognitive computing rest on a distinctive technological know-how groundwork and we endorse that the two foundations are related, but in addition fundamentally distinct. So, we have got a "floor reality" based on particular trends and improvements within the science environment.

For example, there is little dispute that significant information is a phenomenon of the evolution of digital technological know-how throughout consumer, business, government, and scientific lifestyles (and almost every other existence you care so as to add).

At the same time, Cognitive Computing has been related to bringing computing machines to play in such challenges as bringing "human-like" insights to Jeopardy game taking part in, making personal digital assistants smart, accelerating human genome evaluation, and bettering scientific outcomes through prognosis and cure strategies.

All of those examples are centered on the cognitive applications capability to process "past-human" quantities of disparate knowledge while analyzing and offering suggestive, non-trivial, well-timed solutions.

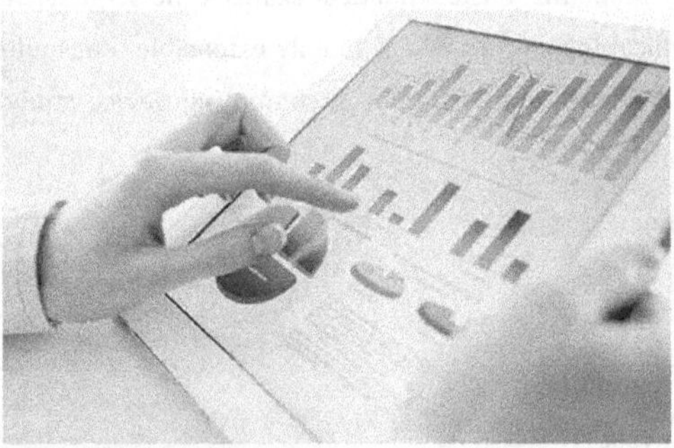

Figure 26: Technology Foundations

Source:http://learnonline.kennesaw.edu/images/courses/information-technology-box.jpg

Cognitive Computing makes a brand new category of problems computable. It addresses difficult situations which can be characterized via ambiguity and uncertainty in one of a kind words, it handles human sorts of troubles. In these dynamic, knowledge-rich and changing circumstances, information tends to alter more commonly, and it is almost always conflicting. The goals of customers evolve as they gain more knowledge and redefine their objectives. To reply to the fluid nature of users figuring out of their problems, the Cognitive Computing procedure presents a synthesis now, not just of information sources, also of impacts, contexts, and insights."

3.7.5. Symbiotic Functions

Even as we have been focusing on the differences of big data and Cognitive Computing in both the task and the science phases, we additionally wish to highlight the valuable relationship between the two traits.

The main relationship between the two is that the availability of big data-scale quantities of data are extremely valuable for types of machine-learning algorithms and methodologies on which Cognitive Computing is dependent for accuracy and contextual appropriateness of its answers or solutions and recommendations. The flipside of this value of increased power of analysis for cognitive applications is off course the brand new types of analytic value these functions offers to those who are seeking to make some form of sense out the petabytes, exabytes or zetta bytes of data that are accrued of their corporation massive facts "lakes" or black.

Figure 27: Symbiotic Functions

Source:http://araignee-pc.com/wp-content/uploads/2016/11/Business-Consultant-.png

Big data and Cognitive Computing will continue to be interrelated and could continue to be spoken approximately together as though they have been a group. Let us turn then to look at other differences, as well as, the interrelationships between the trends and the terms at the functional and symbolic levels.

On the level of characteristic, confusion arises right now from the numerous statements we are able to examine which appear to wrap big data and Cognitive Computing into the same phenomenon.

3.7.6. Maturing of the Market Place

We turn to now, as to how the phrases "big data" and "Cognitive Computing" are running on the symbolic stage.

We need to recognize first that when terms or phrases become buzz labels for entire new phases in the development of the computing business and the information economy; they take on something of a life of their own.

This new existence within the symbolic surroundings has demonstrated through the years to turn buzz terms into potent sources of confusion and complication as a substitute than lead to understanding.

This is the concern these days with big data and Cognitive Computing.

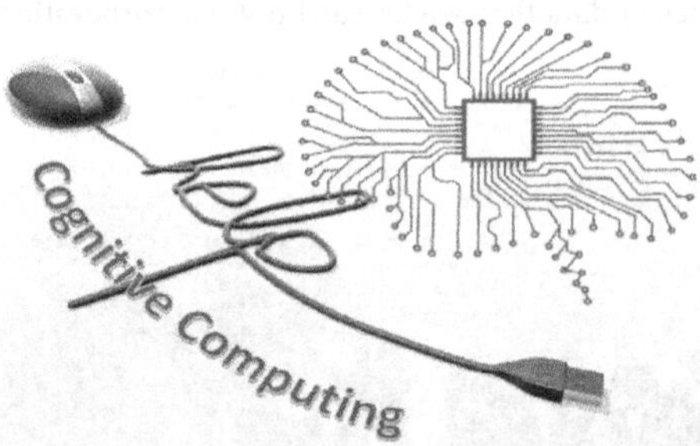

Figure 28: Maturing of the Marketplace

Source: http://www.enterrasolutions.com/media/cognitive-computing-12.png.

For example, simply by looking at the impact of the phenomenon of big data in the marketplace, we see a remarkable difference between the attitude and language of companies who actually run their businesses on big data and those companies who are using these terms but are primarily worried about being left behind.

3.8. Why Cognitive Analytics?

3.8.1. Bring Together the Best of All Worlds

A cognitive system can furnish real-time solutions to questions posed in ordinary language by using looking by way of large quantities of knowledge which have been entered into its capabilities base, making experience of context, and computing the obvious reply. As builders and users "educate" the method, the answers turn out to be more secure and increasingly necessary over time. For example, a healthcare professional can use cognitive analytics to rapidly comb by way of medical journals, clinician notes, patient historical past, and different files to seek out totally relevant information to improve a diagnosis or treatment plan. A call center middle representative can quickly answer a consumer's query about tenting equipment via using a cognitive approach that pulls expertise from product descriptions, patron stories, revenue histories, topical blogs, and travel magazines. Many companies may just decide upon to continue to improve their advanced analytics capabilities, even as cognitive applied sciences continue to conform. However, for firms that must be finding real-time solutions hidden within large amounts of diverse information, cognitive analytics may provide a certain competitive potential.

Figure 29: Cognitive Analytics

Source:https://sctr7.files.wordpress.com/2013/08/data-science-mind.jpg?w=608&h=346.

3.8.2. Other Benefits of Data Analytics

Extract Unused Data Sources

Rather than ignore bulky, diverse data formats, businesses can use cognitive analytics to quickly tap unstructured data, written content documents, pictures, emails, social posts, and more for useful insights.

Provide Personalized Services

Fast, effective service is no longer adequate to win today's customers. Their loyalty is gained through organizations that can provide particularly personalized service based on what the data says about their individual choice and records.

Improve Service Consistency and Quality

Individuals frequently come to different conclusions primarily based upon the identical data. Cognitive analytics can support scale back subjectivity in decision-making and do it faster through finding how choices are made and measuring the ensuing effects, allowing leading practices to be shared across the organization.

Enhance Knowledge Sharing

Cognitive analytics can be utilized to enlarge abilities sharing, offering rapid access to extremely crucial solutions and insights on demand.

Figure 30: Improve Service Consistency and Quality

Source:http://wac.1a76d.edgecastcdn.net/801A76D/analytics/images/site/features/_large/ThinkstockPhotos-518311330.jpg

3.8.3. The Role of Cognition in Data Analysis

Cognitive Science offers a way to understand data analysis at a theoretic level. Concerns of Cognitive Science may seem far from the field of data, but they have precedent in the early works of empirical data analysis. Highlight the role of cognitive processes in their initial descriptions of Exploratory Data Analysis (EDA): "The basic general intent of data analysis is simply stated to - seek through a body of data for interesting relationships and informations and to exhibit the results in such a way as to make them recognizable to the data analyzed," and again, "at all stages of knowledge analysis the character and detail of output, both precise and advantage, should be matched to the capabilities of the individuals who use and need it." Cognitive concerns also appear in recommendations for improving data analysis.

Data analyses rely on the mind's ability to learn, analyze, and understand. Each analysis attempts to educate an observer about some aspect of reality. Usually, this requires data to be manipulated and preprocessed, but the end result of these efforts must be a knowledge product that can be interpreted by the human mind; an analysis cannot be useful if it fails to provide this. Even "black-box" analyses, which may rely on methods that are incomprehensible to the analyst, must produce a result that the analyst can assign meaning to. If they do not, they will not be useful. This last step of assigning meaning is not a statistical or computational step, but a cognitive one. In this way, each data analysis is part of a larger, cognitive task. The success of each data analysis depends on its ability to interact with this cognitive process.

This alone is a good reason for data analysts to learn about cognition; however, cognitive processes also shed insights on the preprocessing stages of a data analysis -- mental processes closely parallel the preprocessing stages of data analyses. Moreover, untrained analysts can and do "analyze" data with only their natural mental abilities.

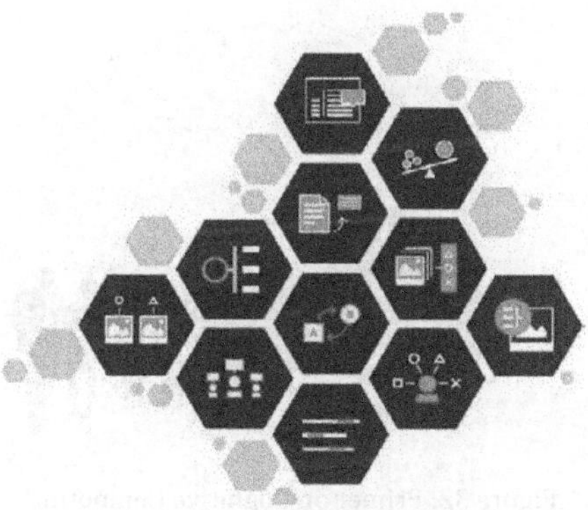

Figure 31: The Role of Cognition in Data Analysis

Source: https://www.ibm.com/watson/assets/img/devcloud.svg

But the analysts like process to create the detailed understanding of bits from the sensory input.

3.8.4. Primer on Cognitive Computing

Latest analytics applied sciences are really adept at analyzing and visualizing historical, structured information. Want to know how many widgets your company sold last quarter by zip code and product line? No problem, there's no shortage of data warehouse and trade intelligence instruments in the marketplace that helps interactive dashboards and different visualizations for this form of job.

But what if you're not just interested in what your company sold, but how your customers feel about your products and your company based on their own words? Not only that, but let's say you also want to predict what products your customers are likely to buy (or not buy) from you next or whether they are likely to agitate to a competitor? And what if you also want recommended actions, steps your company can take, to capitalize on (or prevent) this behavior; that is the place matters get complex.

The real dividing line between these two scenarios is that one requires a backward looking view of a company's own internal data (sales and store location data, for example) and a relatively straightforward visualization tool to display the results. The opposite requires the continuous processing and evaluation of huge volumes of unstructured data and content material (social media streams, news studies, consumer suggestions forms) that results in both predictive (what is likely to happen) and prescriptive (what should I do about it) analytic output.

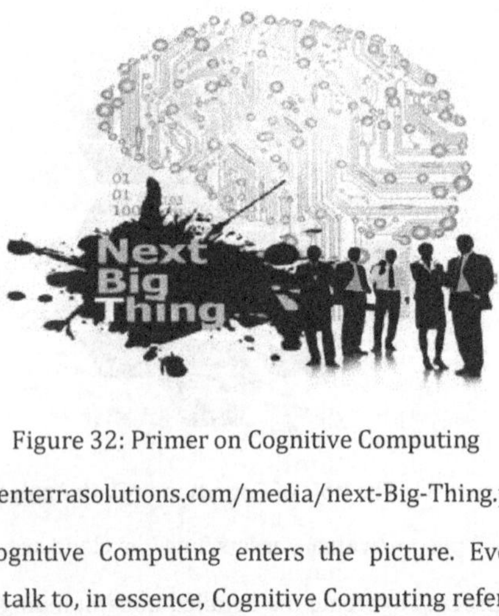

Figure 32: Primer on Cognitive Computing

Source: http://www.enterrasolutions.com/media/next-Big-Thing.png

That is the place Cognitive Computing enters the picture. Even as definitions differ depending on whom you talk to, in essence, Cognitive Computing refers to a kind of developed analytics that attempts to mimic the way the human brain functions; however, at a scale that no single person could achieve. At the same time, Cognitive Computing systems are highly problematic; they all require a couple of foundational constructing blocks to be powerful. These incorporate:

1. **A Large Corpus of Data.** While the form of data depends upon the specifics of the use cases, Cognitive Computing systems require a large quantity of data, more often than not, unstructured written data, upon which to apply analytic methods.

2. **Data Storage and Processing.** All that information has to stay somewhere; this means that Cognitive Computing systems should include a scalable, flexible storage layer.
3. **Machine Learning.** More than required, human interference machine learning algorithms do just overlook, then it replys in the term they learn and familiarize with the results of data analysis to fine tune its model resulting in a closed-loop pointer system.
4. **Natural Language Processing.** Natural language processing (NLP) is an approach of analytics that understand the nuance of human message and can construe verbal words and written facts, in order to perform predictive and prescriptive analytics queries.

Figure 33: Natural Language Processing

Source:http://www.mobilegeeks.com/wp-content/uploads/2016/06/cognitive-computing-the-new-frontier-in-machine-intelligence.jpg

While the concept of Cognitive Computing is not new, a number of developments in the underlying technologies have resulted in significant advancements in Cognitive Computing in present existence.

Particularly, new procedures for significant-scale knowledge processing and storage comparable to Hadoop have made it simpler and more low-cost for Cognitive Computing practitioners to control extremely giant volumes of unstructured data. While, the sheer quantity of unstructured data being created day-to-day is a starting factor, custom machine is required to analyze and write intelligence of the data.

Despite some claims the opposite, most Cognitive Computing systems do not intent to completely swap humans within the resolution-making process. As an alternative, Cognitive Computing approaches complement human choice-making leading to analytic prowess neither Cognitive Computing techniques nor humans would realize on their personal.

3.9. Summary

- Data analytics is the process of examining datasets in order to draw conclusions about the information they contain, increasingly with the aid of specialized systems and software.
- Cognitive analytics is a field of analytics that tries to mimic the human brain by draw inferences from existing data and patterns, draws conclusions based on existing knowledge bases and then inserts this back into the knowledge base for future inferences - a self-learning feedback loop.
- cognitive technologies include computer vision, machine learning, natural language processing, speech recognition, and robotics.
- The difference between the machine learning and cognitive computing are discussed in the next chapter detail.

CHAPTER 4

Machine Learning and Cognitive Systems

4.1. The Next Evolution of Enterprise Intelligence

IBM's recent announcements of three new services based on Watson technology makes it clear that there is pressure in the enterprise software space to incorporate new technologies, both in hardware and software, in order to keep pace with modern business. It seems we are approaching another turning point in technology where many concepts that were previously limited to academic research or very narrow industry niches are now being considered for mainstream enterprise software applications.

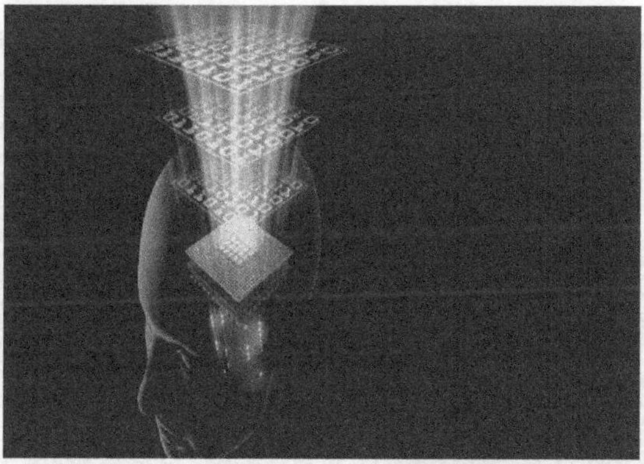

Figure 34: The Next Evolution of Enterprise Intelligence

Source:http://noulpamant.ro/wpcontent/uploads/2012/11/bigstockphoto_the_brain_is_thinking_process_1909054-702x330.jpg

Machine learning, along with many other disciplines within the field of AI and cognitive systems, is gaining popularity, and it may in, the not so distant, future have a colossal impact on the software industry. This first part of series on machine learning explores some basic concepts of the discipline and its potential for transforming the business intelligence and analytics space.

4.1.1. Machine Learning

In simple terms, machine learning is a branch of the larger discipline of AI, which involves the design and construction of computer applications or systems that are able to learn based on their data inputs and/or outputs.

Basically, a machine learning system learns by experience; that is, based on specific training, the system will be able to make generalizations based on its exposition to a number of cases and then be able to perform actions after new or unforeseen events. The discipline of machine learning also incorporates other data analysis disciplines, ranging from predictive analytics and data mining to pattern recognition. And a variety of specific algorithms are used for this purpose, frequently organized in taxonomies, these algorithms can be used depending on the type of input required (a list of algorithms can be found in Wikipedia based on their type).

As a discipline, machine learning is not new. Initial works and references can be traced back to the early fifties with the works of Alan Turing, Arthur Samuel, and Tom M. Mitchell. And the field has undergone extensive development since that time.

Figure 35: Machine Learning

Source:https://www.cloudirec.com/blog/wp-content/uploads/2017/03/Machine-Learning.jpg

One of the more important applications of machine learning is to automate the acquisition of knowledge bases used by so-called expert systems; systems that aim to emulate the decision-making process of human expertise in a field; however, the scope of its application has been growing. In Application of Machine Learning and Rule Introduction, Langley and Simon review some major paradigms for machine learning scenarios, all based on a very important premise; to improve performance on some task, and the general approach involves finding and exploiting regularities in training data.

The major approaches include using neural networks, case-based learning, genetic algorithms, rule induction, and analytic learning.

While in the past they were applied independently, in recent times these paradigms or models are being used in a hybrid fashion, closing the boundaries between them and enabling the development of more effective models.

The combination of analytic methods can ensure effective and repeatable and reliable results, a required component for practical usage in mainstream business and industry solutions.

According to a research paper *"A Few Useful Things to Know about Machine Learning"*, while the discipline by itself is far from simple, it is based on a simple (but not simplistic) principle:

LEARNING = REPRESENTATION + EVALUATION + OPTIMIZATION

Where

- Representation means the use of a classifier element represented in a formal language that a computer can handle and interpret.
- Evaluation consists of a function needed to distinguish or evaluate the good and bad classifiers.
- Optimization represents the method used to search among these classifiers within the language to find the highest scoring ones.

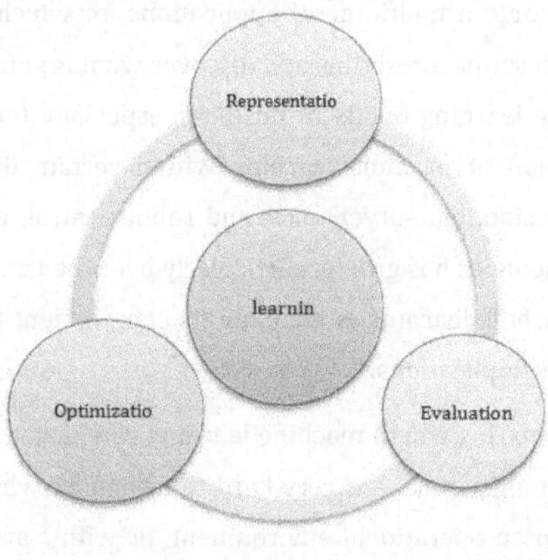

Figure 36: Diagrammatic Representation of Machine Learning

4.1.2. States

The fundamental goal of machine learning is to generalize beyond the examples in the training set. This way the system can infer new decisions or correct answers that then serve to increase learning and optimize accuracy and performance. Also, each component of the machine learning process comprises a good mix of mathematical techniques, algorithms, and methodologies that can be applied.

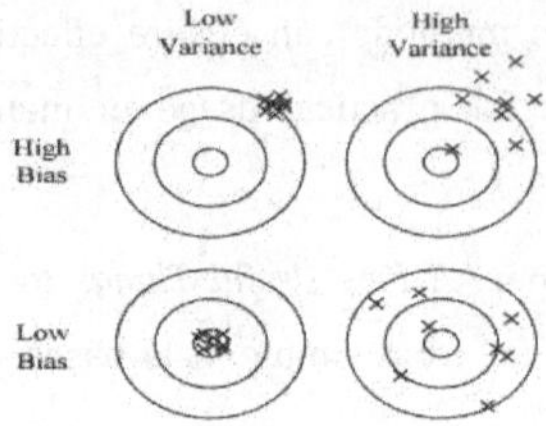

Figure 37: The Three Components of Learning Algorithms

Source: A Few Useful Things to Know about Machine Learning as:

In this context, machine learning can be done by applying specific learning strategies, such

- A supervised strategy to map the data inputs and model them against desired outputs, and
- An unsupervised strategy, to map the inputs and model them to find new trends. Derivative ones that combine these for a semi supervised approach and others are also being used.

This opens the door onto a multitude of applications for which machine learning can be used, in many areas, to describe, prescribe, and discover what is going on within large volumes of diverse data. Machine learning builds in business, especially for analytics-- thanks to the success of the application of machine learning within certain disciplines such as speech recognition, computer vision, bio surveillance, and robot control; the interest in adoption of machine-language technologies has grown, particularly over the last decade. Interesting also is how, in many fields, machine learning is escaping its containment from science labs to reach commercial and business applications.

There are several scenarios where machine learning can have a key role: in those systems that are so complex that algorithms are very hard to design, or when an application requires the software to adapt to an operational environment, or with complex systems that need to work with extensive and complex data sets. In this way, machine learning methods play an increasing role not just in general, in the field of computer science, but also in terms of enterprise software applications, especially for those types of applications that need in-depth data analysis and adaptability. These areas include analytics, business intelligence, and Big Data.

4.2. Business Intelligence and Big Data

An automatic system is being developed to disseminate information to the various sections of any industrial, scientific or government organization. This intelligence system will utilize data-processing machines for auto-abstracting and auto-encoding of documents and for creating interest profiles for each of the "action points" in an organization. Both incoming and internally generated documents are automatically abstracted, characterized by a word pattern, and sent automatically to appropriate action points.

There are several scenarios where machine learning can have a key role: in those systems that are so complex that algorithms are very hard to design, or when an application requires the software to adapt to an operational environment, or with complex systems that need to work with extensive and complex data sets.

In this manner, gadget gaining knowledge of strategies plays an increasing role no longer as on the trendy area of Computer Science; however, additionally in phrases of employer software programs, specifically for the forms of applications that need in-intensity statistics analysis and adaptableness. These areas encompass analytics, business intelligence, and Big Data.

The premise of Business Intelligence (BI) systems has remained pretty much the same: to collect an organization's data from disparate sources and process it in the best possible way to produce useful information and perhaps this is the most important part -- help decision makers to make the best informed decision for the benefit of an organization. A simple definition, not a simple task.

In this regard, BI has been adapting and evolving with extra or lesser degrees of accuracy and failure to offer information people with the capability to make those decisions, and has played a very vital role in the decision help platform of many agencies.

This evolution has modified the role of BI systems not just to provide high-level decision support at a strategic level, but to inform an increasing number of areas involved with middle management and operations.

It has also has improved the need for bi-structures and projects to evolve in the order that they are able to cope with more and more complicated facts, evaluation troubles. Applications need to be boosted so that they can deal with larger and complex amounts of data and can not only provide current status results, but also predict, play with hypothetical scenarios, and finally discover ways to make accurate suggestions --a green field for machine learning.

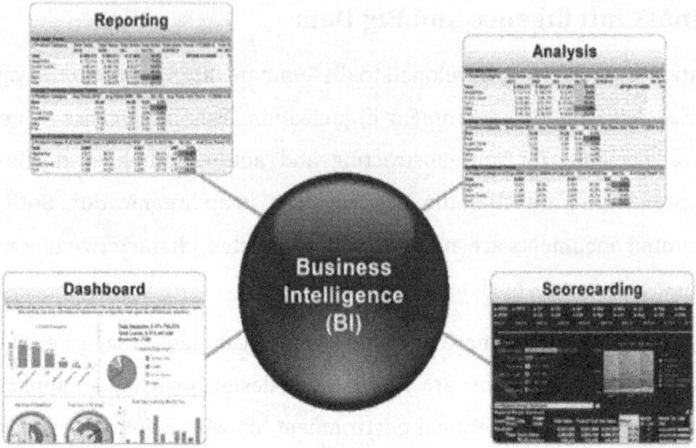

Figure 38: Some Factors Triggering the Need for Faster, Better, and Improved Ways for Decision Support, Analytics, and BI Systems

Source:<http://dssresources.com/history/dsshistory.html>

A good model to understand the evolution of BI systems is D. J. Power's history of decision support systems which of course BI is an important part of.

Decision support systems and applications have evolved in the following stages:

4.2.1. Model Driven

Emphasizes gets admission to and manipulation of financial, optimization and/or simulation models. Simple quantitative models offer the maximum level of functionality. Use restricted data and parameters provided by decision makers to aid decision makers in studying a scenario, but in general huge databases are not needed for model-driven.

4.2.2. Data Driven

In general, a data-driven DSS emphasizes gets right entry to and manipulation of a time series of inner business enterprise information and occasionally outside and actual time information.

Simple file systems accessed through question and retrieval equipment provide the maximum primary degree of functionality. Data warehouse systems that permit the manipulation of data with the aid of computerized tools tailored to a specific venture and placing or via greater general tools and operators. Data-Driven DSS with On-line Analytical Processing (OLAP) provide the best level of capability and selection aid, this is related to evaluation of large collections of old data.

4.2.3. *Communications Driven*

Communications-driven DSS uses community and communications technology to facilitate selection applicable collaboration and conversation. In those systems, communiqué technology are the dominant architectural issue. Tools used encompass groupware video conferencing and PC-based bulletin boards.

Document Driven

Uses computer storage and processing technologies to offer file retrieval and analysis. Large report databases may additionally consist of scanned documents, hypertext documents, snapshots sounds and videos.

Examples of documents that are probably accessed by way of a document driven DSS are regulations and processes, product specs, catalogs and corporate historical documents, including minutes of convention and correspondence. A seek engine is a primary choice aiding tool associated with a record driven DSS. These systems have additionally been called text-oriented DSS.

4.2.4. *Knowledge Driven*

Knowledge-driven DSS can endorse or suggest movements to managers. These DSS are individual PC systems with specialized problem-fixing knowledge. The "expertise" consists of knowledge about a particular domain, expertise of troubles inside that area, and "skill" at fixing a number of these issues.

Within those descriptions there are clear elements in vicinity to decorate the adoption of technology and methodologies along with device learning -- collaboration, intensive management, and increase of non-conventional data (relational).

The want for structures to solve complexity coincides with the appearance of phenomena along with big statistics and superior analytics in business giving a natural space for machine learning to make the doorway to help crunching big sets of complex data, and to be part of the increasingly complex machinery in place for data analysis and decision making.

Along with disciplines like data mining, natural language processing, and others, machine learning is being seen in business as a tool of choice for transforming what use to be a business intelligence application approach into a wider enterprise intelligence or analytics platform or ecosystem, which goes beyond the traditional scope of bi-target on answering "what goes on with enterprise" to present all viable solutions to "why are we doing what we are doing" and "how are we able to do."

As businesses models are becoming more complex and producing massive amounts of data to be handled with less and less latency, decision support, BI systems are required to grow in complexity and in their ability to handle those volumes of data. This call for is boosting the increase of greater state-of-the-art answers to address unique enterprise and enterprise problems. It is no longer sufficient to sit out a truthful result, systems need to provide business guidance.

Some scenarios where machine learning is gaining increased popularity in the context of analytics and BI can be found in applications for risk analysis, marketing analytics, and advanced analytics for huge Data sources.

4.3. Machine Learning is a Reality for Business

As Tim Negris, an Algorithms, Artificial Intelligence and Data Mining expert states in "*Getting Ready for Machine Learning:*" "And it's being increasingly adopted within many analytics, Big Data, and business intelligence initiatives in the form of a component laying side-to-side with other analytics solutions, or packaged inside an answer that has already followed it as part of its functional stack. In either case, machine learning is getting ready to be a part of the subsequent evolution of employer intelligence".

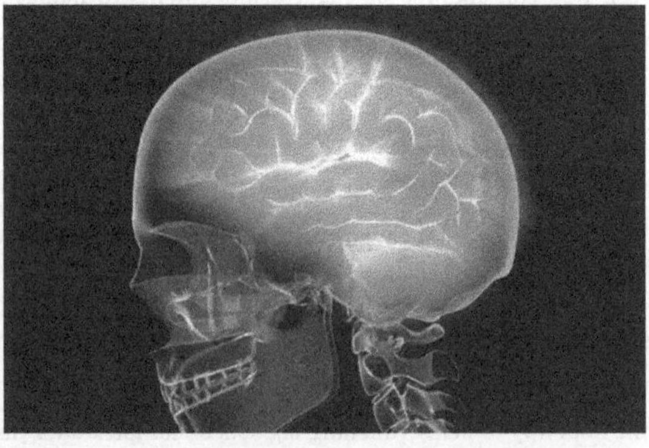

Figure 39: Cognitive Systems - Next Evolution

Source:https://www.wired.com/insights/2014/07/machine-learning-cognitive-systems-next-evolution-enterprise-intelligence-part/

During the last 5 years several techniques had been proposed for managing nonlinear constraints, the usage of evolutionary algorithms (EAs) for numerical optimization problems. Recent survey papers classify those methods into four classes: Upkeep of feasibility penalty functions, searching for feasibility and different hybrids.

The brand new approach for solving constrained numerical optimization issues which includes a homomorphous mapping between n-dimensional cube and a viable seek area. This method constitutes an instance of the fifth decoder based totally on the magnificence of constraint managing techniques. We demonstrate the power of this new approach on several test cases and discuss its further potential suggestions:

- The search string needs to contain some keywords that are not stop words.
- Make sure all terms are spelled correctly.
- Try different terms.
- Try more general terms.
- Try fewer terms.
- Placing "NOT" at the beginning of a search query is not supported unless you are searching within previous search results.

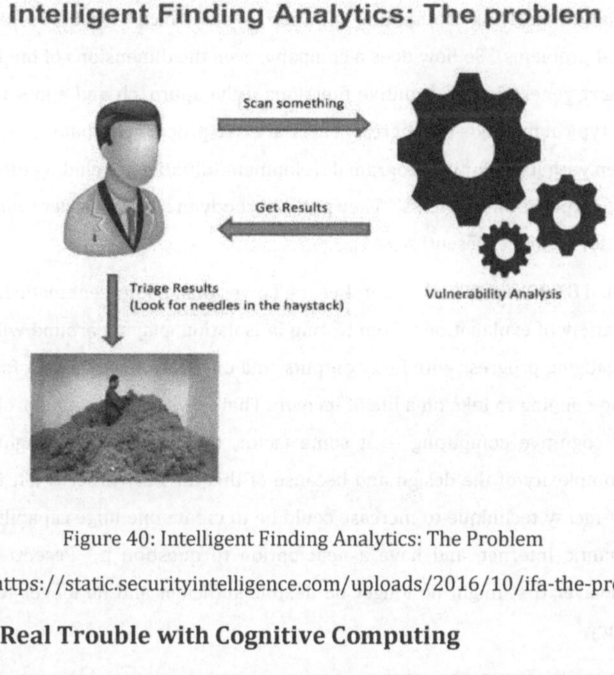

Figure 40: Intelligent Finding Analytics: The Problem

Source:https://static.securityintelligence.com/uploads/2016/10/ifa-the-problem.jpg

4.4. The Real Trouble with Cognitive Computing

One look at the IBM technology roadmap reveals that future emphasis, particularly on the software and applications side, will revolve around that catch-all trend that couples various elements from speech, text, and image recognition to create a brain-like system with reasoning and judgment capabilities–not to mention near-instant access to the world's information.

This action is, of path, jointly referred to as Cognitive Computing and the capabilities accumulated under the wide utility umbrella are discovering a method into extra corporation environments, most especially in well being care. The Watson division at IBM, which is pushing the evolution of clever machines and software by way of new algorithmic advancements, sees the path, evidently in terms of the value these systems will provide–but pushing programs to adapt, in particular algorithmically, is proving to be relatively a task. Apparently, the real problems companies like IBM have little knowledge to do with rough technology limits and are more based around next-new release development, challenges on systems that are evolving extensively and at a price that development cycles are struggling to maintain computer. "In relation to neural networks, we don't thoroughly understand how they work," explains Jerome Pesenti, vice president of the Watson workforce at IBM. "And what's strong is that we're starting to build the programs we are able to utterly understand. The maths and the behavior are fitting very difficult and suspicion is that as we create these networks which might be ever better and hold throwing computing power to it, which creates some interesting methodological problems." So how does a company, even the dimensions of big Blue, go about pushing the next generation of cognitive functions if the approach and application evolution are outpacing typical methods to progress. There are two procedures that IBM was once left to decide between with its cognitive program development initiatives, including those who back a vast variety of corporation segments. "They put everybody in a room earlier than the Jeopardy experiments," for instance, Pesenti says.

"That yielded 8,000 experiments over 4 years. Lower than 20 percent made it."Pesenti says that is for a variety of explanations, from testing in isolation, playing around with algorithmic interactions, gauging progress with fuzzy outputs, and of course, checking out for bugs in code that used to be opening to take on a life of its own. That is where the actual problem lies with the future of cognitive computing -- at some factor, the progress will ought to meet the algorithmic complexity of the design and because of this the only process left is the "messy" one. "The non-messy technique to increase could be to create one huge capabilities model, as with the semantic internet, and have a neat option to question it," Pesenti tells the next Platform. "However that might no longer be flexible sufficient and no longer furnish enough insurance policy.

So we're left with the messy method.

As an alternative of taking knowledge and structuring it in one position, it's a topic of preserving data sources as they are and there is not any silver bullet algorithm to make use of on this case either.

All has to be mixed, from average language processing, computer studying, skills, examples. The next, which meshed as some style of disbursed infrastructure."What IBM ended up thus of the iterative and to some measure, failure-based method to melding multiple algorithms, utility areas, and talents sets, looks anything like what Pesenti shares below, but this distributed architecture will have to proceed to expand for area-particular wishes, not to point out for additional development of cognitive capabilities inside IBM's Watson study organizations.

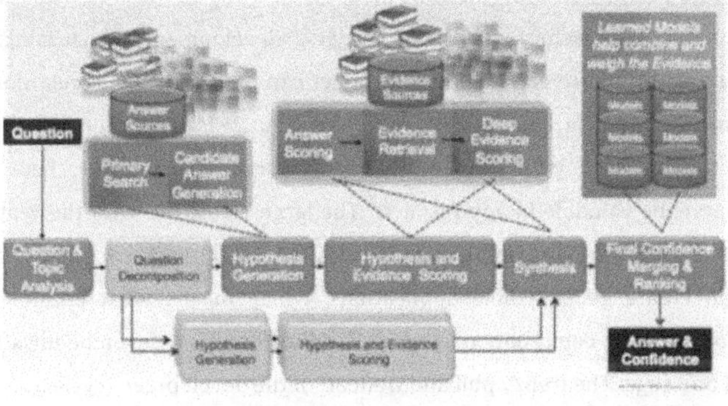

Figure 41: Real Trouble with Cognitive Computing

Pesenti has encountered the unknown with development cycles earlier than, including most famously with the development of novel search engine (for the time) technology by way of the startup Vivisimo, which was on cespunout of work at Carnegie Mellon college.

The startups speed search functionality used to be the backend for a number of federal tasks within the U.S. and served because the manufacturers search backbone for a quantity of gigantic corporations. IBM bought the enterprise in 2012 to add to their giant knowledge portfolio before packaging up the technology to move into the Watson crew's circles quickly thereafter. He notes that the "test all" strategy could not have labored with a smaller crew; it takes the huge, combined effort of many researchers with the freedom to experiment and fail and that needs to be a tough information for startup companies looking to put together comprehensive methods that may reap enough algorithmic and source complexity to thrive.

Past remarking on the unsettling fact that there is an unaided development of cognitive capabilities, pushed forth by ever-extra unique function recognition and linking, the question becomes how Cognitive Computing will grow if the program development is outpaced by using the intelligence of the systems.

Whilst Pesenti does not see this as a crisis yet, per se, it has already created research and progress chasms which are inflicting the Watson teams to propose about how they will enhance the subsequent generation of cognitive functions. And from a system difficulty point of view, groups throughout the Watson staff are heading again to the "throw it all in opposition to a wall to peer what sticks" paradigm. This implies a variety of failure, a lot of "wasted" research, but ultimately, the small percent of successes make it worthwhile from an IBM R&D investment point of view. While an enterprise like IBM, principally in its study division, can put collectively large companies of bright minds and throw away as much as eighty percentage of what rolls out that belief factory, spurring this style of development (which is based on failure, trying out, and extra failure earlier than a product can rear its head) is just not sensible for many corporations. And further, says Pesenti, "The venture is seeing the higher image inside these exams and disasters with so many relocating parts, what seems to be a hit would no longer, I observe, be valuable in any respect." The largest obstacle with the Watson progress cycle too is that teams are not simply fixing issues for one distinct discipline. As a substitute, they ought to create generalizable applications, which means what possibly is good for healthcare, for example, could now not be a just right fit and may even be unsafe to a subject like financial offerings. The frenzy pull and tradeoff of the development cycle as a result always hindered by way of this and is the key barrier for businesses any smaller than an IBM, Google, Microsoft, and other giants.

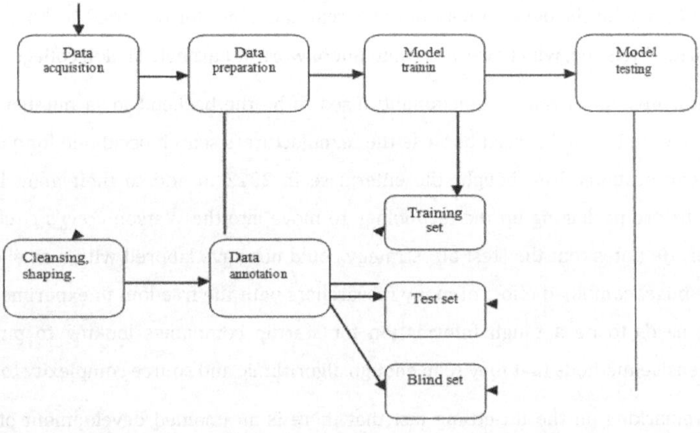

Figure 42: Flow Chart for Real Trouble with Cognitive Computing

Source:https://image.slidesharecdn.com/codemash-machinelearningwithapachespark-160119152043/95/machine-learning-with-apache-spark-14-638.jpg?cb=1453217004

4.5. Thinking Big with Cognitive Computing

4.5.1. The Current State of Play

Cognitive Computing is the CNS of the nascent crop of six innovative technologies and products, forming the key factor to understand humans, matters, hobbies, and the environment.

Imbued with the capacity to simulate human intelligence and effectually process fuzzy information and issues, cognitive computing can also be main for data analysis and decision-making certainly, cognitive systems are information systems that contain the cognitive hallmarks of learning, inferring, deducing, and computing.

Research in Cognitive Computing has long gone by means of a few ups and downs in each momentum and progress. Colossal achievements in fields such as databases and informed systems, for example, had been counterbalanced by means of hindrances in desktop translation and typical language processing. Due to the fact that entering the twenty first century, large knowledge and high-efficiency computing have pushed Cognitive Computing into a pleasant time marked by using the commercial use of deep learning in speech attention, image, and video. Many corporations, including Google, IBM, Facebook, Microsoft, and Baidu, had been lively in the Cognitive Computing sector, mainly a business upsurge within the area and the speedy emergence of associated technologies. Based on deep learning, machine's cognitive advantage has grown to be on par with humans in areas corresponding to face recognition and image classification, and are correctly extra accurate than the human eye. Equally, the Watson system was once designed under IBM's Deep question-answer challenge to reply to questions from the quiz show Jeopardy and defeated two former winners in 2011.

Brain-inspired computing that uses a mass system of built-in circuits to simulate the behavior of neurons, is marching towards commercialization, with Qualcomm is already planning to use the Zeroth neural community chip to make stronger its cell phone processors.

A series of wonderful developments in the present study and applications for cognitive computing has been accompanied by means of a gradual upward pattern in funding in R&D via ICT businesses. Huawei stands out as probably the most few companies to advance Cognitive Computing plans founded on each the Von Neumann and mind-influenced architectures. Huawei plans to coordinate its resources in quite a lot of areas including communications, network topology, computing, and storage to underpin the public Huawei cognitive cloud platform, Huawei REN.

Huawei believes that sustained technical evolution will create new types of business items that will see the effect of cognitive computing on the industrial sector proceed to grow. Sustained commercial progress is also increasing in software scope and technical upgrades, and cultivating an open and modern ecosystem. Huawei REN is committed to promoting the evolution and progress of cognitive computing in four areas: cloud-pipe-device synergy with layered intelligence, cognitive computing as a service, heterogeneous coordination, and mind-motivated intelligence.

4.5.2. Cloud-Pipe-Device with Layered Intelligence

Layered intelligence is displayed on finish devices through perception and action, on network transmission through planning, and on the cloud through learning and evolution. It's a naturally chosen state of intelligence that humans have attained after 200,000 years of evolution, with the valuable apprehensive method offering a peculiarly excellent example.

Cognitive Studying on a coordinated cloud-pipe-gadget platform is also in contrast to human finding out in type, but it surely is similar in spirit. Memory and cognition are acquired from the cloud, while perception, interplay, and motion control are coordinated on the device. For example, in video evaluation-variety purposes, the end gadget is in charge for wishes perception, initial cognitive analysis, and transmitting the initial analytical outcome to the cloud. The network transmits knowledge, develops an understanding of the kind of service being handled, and provides an analytical forecast. The cloud makes use of a cognitive model and algorithms to investigate the video and return the results to the end device for visual display.

In this example, the device, pipe and cloud perform cognition and processing on video analysis applications from different angles and layers to achieve coordinated, layered intelligence.

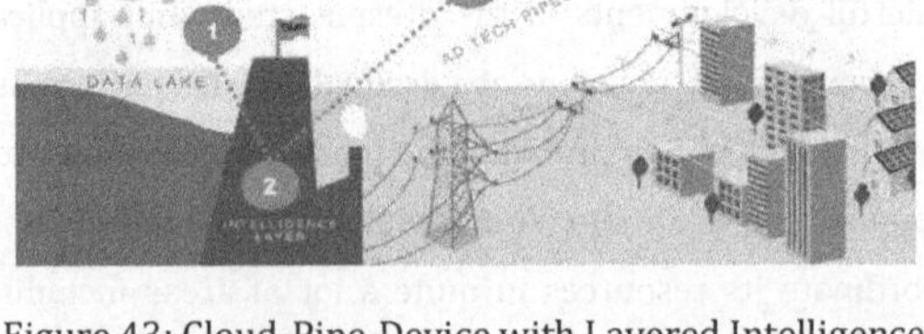

Figure 43: Cloud-Pipe-Device with Layered Intelligence

Source:https://2bd2y2367xnj3kpntjsifzmf-wpengine.netdna-ssl.com/wp-content/uploads/2017/02/chris_ohara1.png

Layered intelligence can be bringing several advantages. Elements of service operation and selection making will shift all the way down to the quit tool and the intelligent network gateway. Both will boost up selections and respectively lessen the sudden shock that perceptual facts create to get right of entry to networks and the surprise that visitors causes on operators' spin networks.

Moreover, a cloud with robust computing and energetic talents allows deep-level research and analysis on perceptual facts and information from wide-ranging areas. It can also discover associations among facts from one of a kind dimension. Combined, these competencies produce the most correct effects of decisions based on evaluation and forecasts from a systemic angle. It also allows data alternate and selections to be adjusted primarily based on the intelligent devices allotted during the course of the device and pipe.

4.6. Cognitive Computing as a Service

Although still in its infancy, the idea of Cognitive Computing as a provider has already gripped the cloud computing marketplace. For example, system translation as a cloud service can translate cellular telephony apps into distinct languages. In the future, service-based cognitive computing will shape a vital development path for cognitive technology and enterprise models, and evolve in an extra refined, granular, and personalized route.

High refinement and granularity denote the ability to perceive spatial and temporal variations in client wishes. Personalization provides layered offerings that concentrate on purchaser needs and problem-areas by way of embedding Cognitive Computing as a service in giving up equipment, devices, and sensors. These are interconnected, and may understand client wishes anywhere and anytime to provide the data and services clients may want.

A study sensible cloud e-assistant offering for on-line businesses reveals clear variations among the requirements that one-of-a-kind kind of online companies have on customer support e-assistants.

For example, an online enterprise for hygienic foods may point out its need for a cloud e-assistant to Huawei REN. Huawei REN would first understand the unique features of services corresponding to hygienic foods, after which provide those capabilities on- line thru a cloud e-assistant with complete know-how about meals, nutrition, and health. The e-assistant could then offers personalized recommendations and automated client services for the next commercial enterprise client. Huawei REN is able to dynamically obtain user feedback in keeping with the consumer's consumption records, and continue to improve the personalization and accuracy of the service.

Cognitive Computing as a service lets in programs to offer an advanced service experience based totally on Cognitive Computing era.

Cognitive structures shape clearly heterogeneous computing environments through distinctive feature of components consisting of CPUs, GPUs, FPGAs, DSPs, and neuron processors, each with their own algorithms and tasks; for example, CPUs are adept at logical operations and GPUs are adept at numerical operations. Cognitive structures can automatically perceive the addresses of the high-level programs based totally upon a priori know-how and historic data.

They can absolutely adapt applications and computing components, and use appropriate components for one-of-a-kind use situation. Current heterogeneous cognitive structures focus on growing cognitive algorithms, meaning that software program engineers use heterogeneous computing additives to boost up the rate of designated algorithms.

The future will see an increasing number of cognitive algorithms based totally on heterogeneous machine design.

Heterogeneous computing is noticeably efficient, requires little power, and is especially useful for Cognitive Computing, where demands on computing assets are high. Heterogeneous coordination can help in the technical evolution of converged software and hardware, and create new paths to comprehend tool-pipe-cloud coordinated intelligence.

4.6.1. Brain-Inspired Intelligence

As the study of Neuroscience has progressed, extra researchers are starting to consider that Cognitive Computing can and needs to attain its ideas from Neuroscience to assist develop new theories and methods, and enhance machine's cognitive expertise of big data. A system both national and worldwide members of the academic world increasingly agree upon, is the use of Turing machines to solve left-brain problems, and mind-inspired computing to solve right-brain problems. Cognitive Computing calls for the left and right sides of the brain to be integrated.

China's Brain Plan is energetic in three most important areas: Shifting past Von Neumann's computing concept and version; making breakthroughs within the form of latest components that evolve computing principle from mathematical models to physical techniques; and huge scale, real-time structures that version human brain.

Brain-stimulated intelligence has the capacity to revolutionize Cognitive Computing and create a new paradigm of self sustaining cognition.

4.6.2. *A Prosperity Generator*

Cognitive Computing systems enjoy extremely large business possibilities, market price, and awareness scenarios, as an example, smart gadgets, smart houses, clever robots, self sufficient vehicles, SMEs, records facilities, and wise workplace automation. They also can be used for economic analysis and gene evaluation, and in the data services of big companies to enable functions which include records retrieval, targeted advertisement drives, mobile medicine, smart transportation, and smart strength grids. After nearly twenty years, Cognitive Computing is in the end developing, we hope that each one, most importantly, ICT groups and studies agencies are enthusiastic about jointly riding the Cognitive Computing technology closer to prosperity.

4.7. Genetic Algorithms and Evolutionary Algorithms – Introduction

Genetic algorithms in Excel to solve optimization problems, by the use of Evolutionary Solver made by Frontline Systems, builders of the "Solver" in Microsoft Excel, known as the Premium Solver Platform.

A genetic or evolutionary algorithm applies the ideas of evolution observed in nature to the problem of finding an assured solution to a Solver problem.

In a "genetic set of rules," the problem is encoded in a chain of bit strings that are manipulated via the set of rules; in an "evolutionary set of rules," the decision variables and problem functions are used directly. Most commercial Solver products are based totally on evolutionary algorithms.

An evolutionary algorithm for optimization isn't the same as "classical" optimization techniques in several ways:

- Random Versus Deterministic Operation.
- Population Versus Single Best Solution.
- Creating New Solutions Through Mutation.
- Combining Solutions Through Crossover.
- Selecting Solutions Via "Survival of the Fittest".
- Drawbacks of Evolutionary Algorithms.

Randomness

First, it is based on a component on random sampling. This makes it a nondeterministic technique, which might also yield fairly exclusive solutions on extraordinary runs even though haven't modified model.

In comparison, the linear, nonlinear and integer Solvers , they are protected by using the Premium Solver, and are deterministic technique and they are continually yield the same answer in case start with the same values in the choice variable cells.

Population

Second, in which maximum classical optimization methods hold a single best answer determined so far, an evolutionary algorithm continues a population of individual answers. Only one (or some, with equivalent goals) of those is "fine," but the other participants of the population are "pattern factors" in other areas of the search area, wherein a better solution may additionally later be discovered.

The use of a population of answers facilitates the evolutionary set of rules to keep away from becoming "trapped" at a proximate reliable answer, whilst an excellent higher most reliable answer may be located outside the area of the current answer.

Mutation

Third - inspired with the aid of the function of mutation of an organism's DNA in human evolution - an evolutionary algorithm periodically makes random adjustments or mutations in a single or extra participants of the modern-day population, yielding a brand new individual solution (which may be higher or worse than present population individuals). There are many feasible approaches to carry out a "mutation," and the Evolutionary Solver truly employs 3 distinct mutation techniques.

The end result of a mutation may be an infeasible answer, and the Evolutionary Solver attempts to "repair" this kind of strategy to make it feasible; this is every so often, but no longer constantly, a hit.

Crossover

Fourth - inspired through the position of sexual reproduction in the evolution of living things - an evolutionary set of rules attempts to mix factors of current answers so that it will create a brand new solution, with a number of the features of every "discern." The elements (e.g., the decision variable values) of existing answers are combined in a "crossover" operation, inspired through the crossover of DNA strands that happens in reproduction of biological organisms.

As with mutation, there are many feasible ways to carry out a crossover operation - a few a good deal higher than others - and the Evolutionary Solver truly employs a couple of variations of two distinct crossover techniques.

Selection

Fifth-- inspired by the position of natural choice in evolution --an evolutionary set of rules perform a spread system wherein the "most fit" participants of the population survive, and the "least fit" members are removed. In a constrained optimization problem, the perception of "fitness" depends partly on whether a solution is feasible (i.e., whether it satisfies all of the constraints), and partially on its objective feature cost. The selection process is the step that guides the evolutionary set of rules in the direction of ever-higher solutions.

Drawbacks

A disadvantage of any evolutionary set of rules is that an answer is "higher" nearest in comparison to other, currently recognized solutions; such a set of rules certainly has no idea of an "assured solution," or any way to check whether a solution is optimum. (For this purpose, evolutionary algorithms are high-quality used for problems in which it is difficult or impossible to check for optimality). This additionally means that an evolutionary set of rules never knows for certain when to anticipate, other than the length of time, or the quantity of iterations or individual solutions, that wish to allow it to explore.

4.8. Summary

- Machine learning involves the design and construction of computer applications or systems that are able to learn based on their data inputs and outputs.
- The principle of machine learning defines that learning is a combination of representation, evaluation and optimization.
- The fundamental goal of machine learning is to generalize beyond the examples in the training set.
- In the next chapter we are going to discuss about emerging evolution in cognitive computing applications.

CHAPTER 5

Emerging Evolution in Cognitive Computing Application

5.1. Affective Computing (AC)

It is defined as the study, the development of the system and the device that can able to recognize, interpret, process and simulates the human effects. It is a multidisciplinary field that integrates with Computer Science, Cognitive Science and Psychology.

This technique was explored by Rosalind Picard 1995 on paper affective computing for the ability of empathy. In affective computing, the machine must interpret with the emotions of the humans and should adapt its behavior with them, and gives an appropriate response to those emotions.

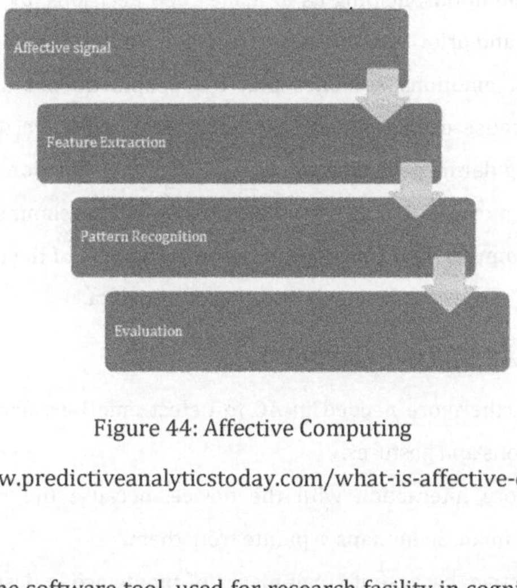

Figure 44: Affective Computing

Source: http://www.predictiveanalyticstoday.com/what-is-affective-computing/

Software Tool

MIT Media Lab is the software tool, used for research facility in cognitive states, especially through creation of wearable sensors with new machine learning algorithm. It leads to find a new technique to access frustration, stress and emotions indirectly, by using natural interaction and conversation.

5.1.1. Labs in Affective Computing

MIT Media Lab

It combines Engineering and Computer Science with Psychology, Cognitive Science, Neuro science, and more.

Microsoft Vibe

VIBE, full form stands for the Visualization and Interaction for Business and Entertainment. It focuses mainly on emotion tools and emotion tracking.

5.1.2. Goals of the Affective Computing

- Used to sense and react respectfully to human emotions. For instance, if the person was communicating with the technology and he/she is frustrated or confused, the technology needs to be enabled to respond differently to that person. If the humans respond differently to the technology, the technology should do the same.
- Another goal of AC was to enable people to communicate their emotions more clearly. Itisimportanttolookthattheemotionplaysaroleequallyintheintelligenceprocess.
- AC, describes about how they understand that emotion plays a vital role with us to regulate our intentions, helping us to make good decisions, by changing the way that we emphasize and prioritize things, organizing or finding out what matters.
- These roles of emotions are ones that the people do not usually think about as emotional, because usually we are not 'emotional' when we do that, it is just some background regular mechanisms that are important for functioning intelligently.
- By using this purpose to increase their quality of the communication between the human and computer, and also improve the intelligences of the computer, AC builds an "affect model" based on a various sensors-captured data.

5.1.3. Limitations of Affective Computing

- Research is furthermore needed in AC to detect emotions from videos, audio, texts, facial expressions and gestures.
- People get more interaction with the device, because the robot can identify the emotion of a human. So humans separate from them.
- Very cost effective, because if small pieces of the device is destroyed, it is difficult to manufacture it.
- It is difficult to identify all emotions of the human being.

5.1.4. Top Companies in Affective Computing

Affectiva

Affectiva technology enables to track user's smile and frowns by using the webcam and also used for measuring the user's amusement, surprise and confusion. It can even able to measure their heart rate by using only a webcam.

Realeyes

Using webcam can easily measure the user's reaction during watching the video. Here some of the examples of realeyes represented in the graphical representation.

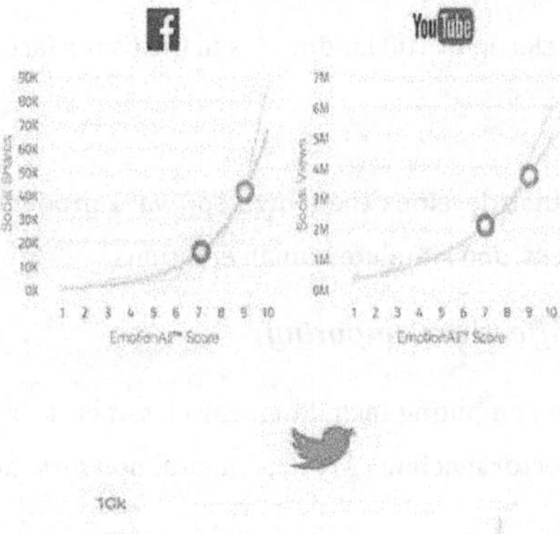

Figure 45: Graphical Representations of the Realeyes Technique

Source:http://www.predictiveanalyticstoday.com/what-is-affective-computing/

Emotient

Emotient is a cloud- based service developer delivers direct measurements of the customer and audience's unfiltered emotional response to advertisements, contents, product or sales/service interaction. It provides the complete, accurate facial expression and frame by frame measurements of nine key emotions.

Beyond Verbal

It was developed to recognize emotion from human voice.

Sension

Sension builds face tracks up to 100 landmark's in the user's face.

tACC

It is an AC company that develops their own software products and provide services to recognize, interpret, process, and simulate human emotions.

5.1.5. Algorithms in Affective Computing

Algorithms in affective computing include Linear classifier, k- nearest neighbor algorithm, Mixture model, Support vector machine, Artificial neural network, decision tree algorithm, and Hidden Markov model.

Linear Classifier

LDC classification happens to the value which is based on the linear combination for the future values which was provided in the vector features.

K-nearest Neighbor Algorithm

Classification happens by locating the object in future spaces and comparing it with k-nearest neighbor.

Support Vector Machine

SVM is the type of the linear classifier that decides by which of the two possible cases is available from the information source.

Artificial Neural Network

ANN is the mathematical model inspired by the biological network that can better grasp the non-linearity of their feature space.

Decision Tree Algorithm

It works based on following decision tree model which leaves can represent the classification outcome and the branches represent the conjunction of subsequent features that leads to the classifications.

Hidden Markov Model

HMM is the Statistical Markov model in which the states and state transitions are not directly available for observations. Instead the series of the output dependents on the states are visible.

Mixture Model

GMM is a probability model used to represent the existence of sub-population within the overall population. Each population was described by using their mixture distribution, which permits to do further of their classification of observations to sub-populations.

5.2. Analytics

Cognitive Analytics is a term used to describe how the organization applies analytics and cognitive computing to help humanity to take smarter decisions. Cognitive Analytic is a field of analytic that tries to mimic the human brain by drawing interference from existing data and pattern, drawing conclusions which are based on existing knowledge bases for future interference - a self learning future loop.

A cognitive system can provide the real-time answers to the questions posted in any language by searching through the massive amount of information that have been sourced from its knowledge base, making the sense of its context, and it executes the most related answers.

The Cognitive analytics and solutions department develops the advanced Cognitive Computing, with analytics techniques, explores with the human aspects of cognitive computing and develops innovative solutions for the various industries.

The department specializes in handling data of all types, ranging from the exact traditional structured data to semi-structured data, such as logos, text data, social networks, audio, images and video.

In a particular stage, the department develops their novel of the analytic solutions to extract information from this data and to augment with the human cognition in variety of domains, including healthcare, life science, Telco, commerce, and enterprise knowledge management. As developers and users train the system, the answers become more reliable and increases value over the time. For example, a doctor can quickly go through medical journals, clinician notes, patient history, and other documents to find highly relevant information to improve their diagnosis or treatment given to them by using the cognitive analytics.

A call center representatives can answer to the customer very quickly by using cognitive analytics question about the camping gear, that shows information from product description, customer ranking, detailed sales history, topical blogs, and travel magazines.

Many organizations might choose this technique to continue and develop their advanced analytics capability while cognitive technologies continue to evolve.

But for organizations they need to find the real-time answers hidden within massive amounts of diverse data, cognitive analytics may provide a distinct competitive advantage.

5.2.1. *Advantages of Cognitive Analytics*

Helpful to Find Untapped Data Sources

Rather than ignore bulky, diverse data formats, organizations can use this cognitive analytics to help quickly find ways to tap unstructured information, text, documents, images, emails, social posts, and use it for more insights in information.

Use to Provide Personalized Services

Fast and efficient service is no longer enough to meet the needs of the today's consumers. Their loyalty of the department is won by their organization providing highly personalized service based on what the data says about their individual preferences and history.

To Improve Service Quality and Consistency

Humans usually come to know about different conclusions based on the same information. Cognitive analytics help us to reduce the subjectivity in the decision making, and do it at a faster rate by tracing how decisions are made and by measuring their resulting outcomes, allowing leading practices to be shared across the organization.

To Improve Knowledge Sharing

It can be used to boost the knowledge sharing, provides fast access to highly related answers and insights on demand.

5.2.2. *Limitations of Cognitive Analytics*

- Reduces human power. Since the device can translate or analyse any language, speech from. Any audio or video data, there is no need for human involvement.
- Not very cost effective, if the part or piece of the device is destroyed. It is difficult to reproduce it.

5.2.3. *Requirement of Cognitive Analytics*

Cognitive Analytics requires four major capabilities:

- **Collection**: The ability to find and get related information from a variety of sources, and a variety of forms.
- **Context**: The ability which helps to find the implicitly or explicitly extract features and relationships from different data and data sources, and producing metadata to randomly build an updated context around the data.
- **Elements Cognition**: The analysis of data within a variety of contextual data, delivering understanding and insights about the information and metadata (e.g., relationships).
- **Exploitation**: The application of Collection, Context and Cognition to guide actions – e.g., decision support or automation.

5.2.4. *Cognitive Analytic Architecture*

The below Figure 46 describes about the software architecture of IBM content analytical. The crawler Framework was used to find the nature of the data. It uses an IBM search engine that can able enlarge for efficient storage information.

The first phase uses the data from the knowledge management and generally the source data may not be available due to the organization terms and the policies.

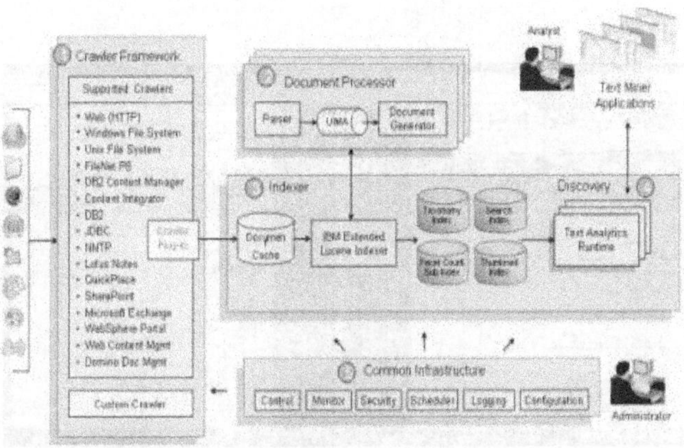

Figure 46: Cognitive Analytic Architecture

Source: IBM Research, "Neuro synaptic Chips, Building Blocks for Cognitive Computing," http://www.research.ibm.com/cognitivecomputing/neurosynaptic-chips.shtml

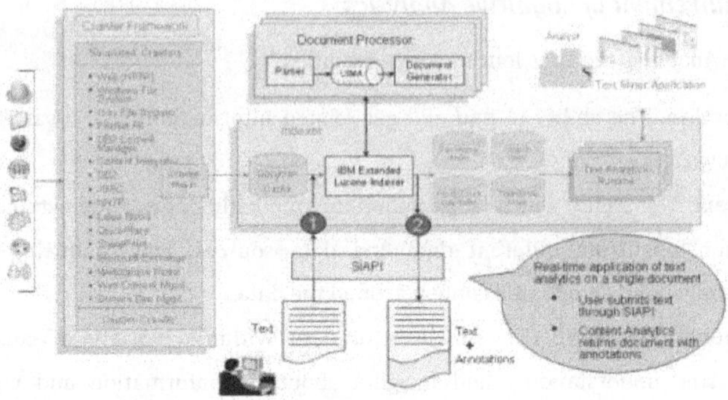

Figure 47: Contextual Analytic Component

Source: IBM Research, "Neurosynaptic Chips, Building Blocks for Cognitive Computing," http://www.research.ibm.com/cognitivecomputing/neurosynaptic-chips.shtml

The second phase involves analyzing the data individually and applying for the various data formats. This technique is used to check the implicit or explicit data-extracted output data. It is also used to check the related information between the diverse data from the source data. The Search Index and API used to identify one from the multiple documents in resulting annotation. Annotation supports an array of analytical processing capabilities such as language identification part of speech identification, tagging, part of speech tagging with the video and more.

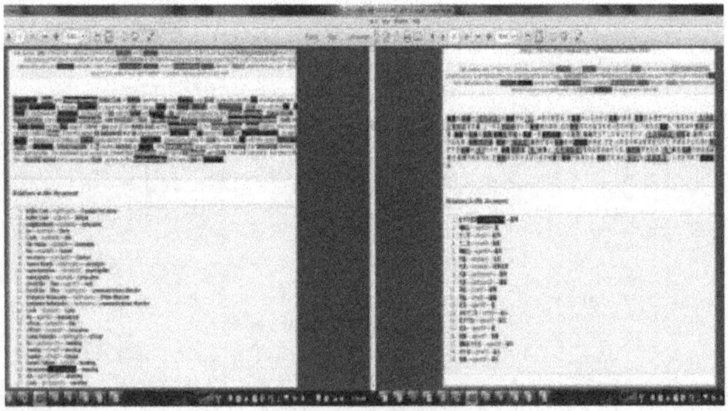

Figure 48: Text Analytics

Source: IBM Research, "Neurosynaptic Chips, Building Blocks for Cognitive Computing," http://www.research.ibm.com/cognitivecomputing/neurosynaptic-chips.shtml

In the above figure 48 the list of keywords were illustrated and the color coded to easily identify with the user. By using this analytics it was able to identify the multiple spelling of the same name, pronounce and the parts of the speech tagging.

IBM extended support to many foreign languages such as English, Arabic, Chinese and Russian. It includes two types of machine translations: Rules Based machine translation and Statical Based Machine translation.

To accomplish this we can use the multimedia annotators. Such as:

- **Language Identifier**: Helpstofind128languagesbyusingthefirstthreephonemes.
- **Speech-to-text translator**: Enables to convert speech-to-text and applying the text analytics.
- **Speaker Identifier**: Helps to find the multiple speakers in an audio or video, and then able to identify a particular speaker.

The below figure 49 describes about its ability to identify the text analytics in multimedia, the newsreader speaking Arabic. The dynamic speech-to-text conversion annotator was presented below her video, and then dynamic translation from Arabic to English in the window below the Arabic.

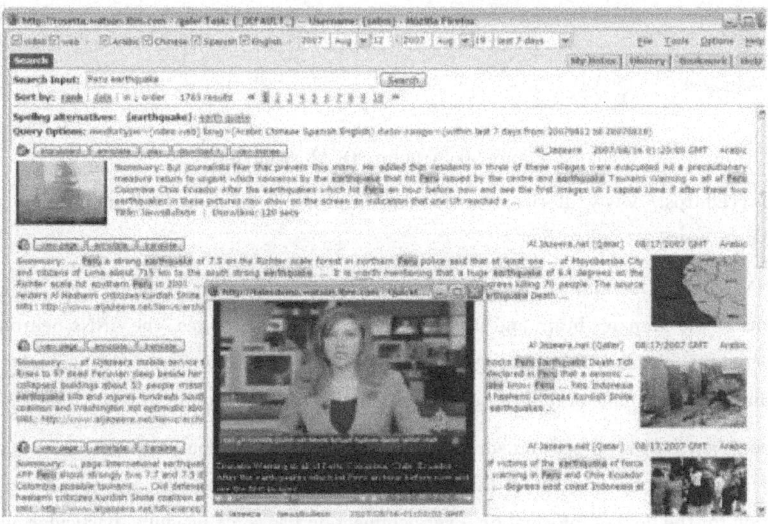

Figure 49: Multimedia Analytics

Source: IBM Research, "Neurosynaptic Chips, Building Blocks for Cognitive Computing," http://www.research.ibm.com/cognitivecomputing/neurosynaptic-chips.shtml

The above figure 49 shows annotated text from an extracted search across data sources including both text and multimedia. An important observation is that this system now enables users to search multimedia natively and apply the same analysis to any combination of structured text, unstructured text, images, audio, and video concomitantly.

5.3. Artificial Neural Network

ANNs are a data processing model which works similar to the brain's neural structure. ANNs are considered as nonlinear statistical modeling tools -- here the complex bond between input and output are modeled clearly and also that the information passed through the networks will affect the structure of the ANNs, because it changes the neural structure based on that input and output.

The connections of ANNs are generally organized in layers. The structure comprises of one input layer, one or more hidden layers and an output layer.

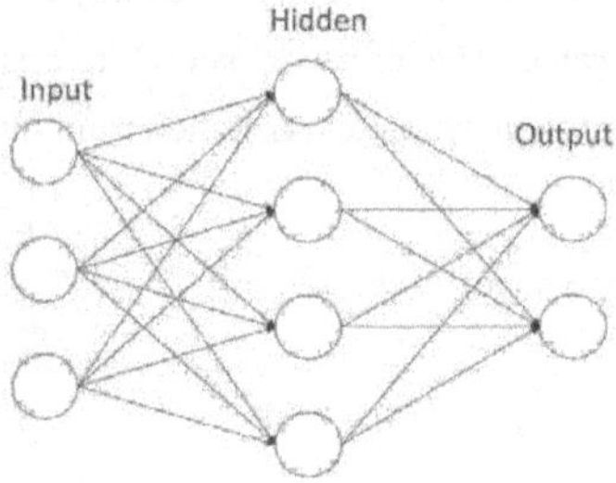

Figure 50: Structure Of ANNs Model

Source:https://www.tutorialspoint.com/artificial_intelligence/artificial_intelligence_neural_networks.htm

ANNs consists of multiple nodes, here the structure basically resembles the biological neurons of the human's brain and it is composed of multiple nodes. The ANNs neurons are connected by links and they exchange information with each other. The nodes will take input data and perform simple or multiple operations on the data in the hidden layer.

Then the result is passed to neurons in the output layer. The output of all nodes is either called node or activation value. Every arrow connects two neurons and it indicates the direction for the flow of information. Every connection has some weight, a particular number which controls the signal between two neurons. If a network produces a desired output, then there is no need for adjusting the weight. In case if the network generates an error or an undesired output, then the system has to alter the weights to improve following results.

5.3.1. Types of ANNs

- FEEDFORWARD
- FEEDBACK

Feed forward

The flow of information in this type is UNIDIRECTIONAL where an acknowledgement is not sent to the unit when an information is received and there will not be any feedback loops. ANNs type is generally used in pattern generation, pattern classification and pattern specification.

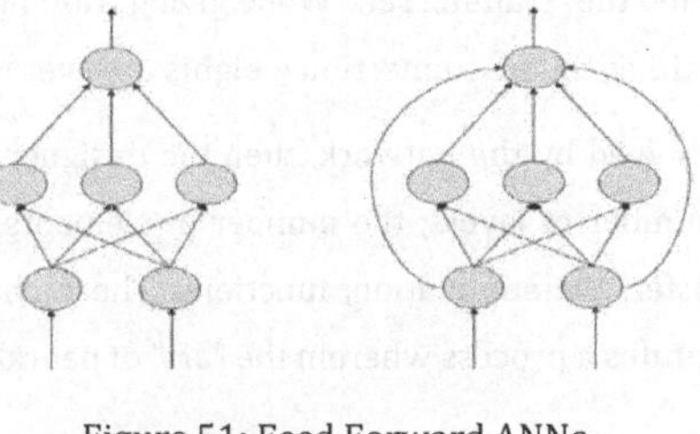

Figure 51: Feed Forward ANNs

Source:https://www.tutorialspoint.com/artificial_intelligence/artificial_intelligence_neural_networks.htm

Feedback

Here, the Feedback or acknowledgement is allowed. They are mostly used in content addressable memories.

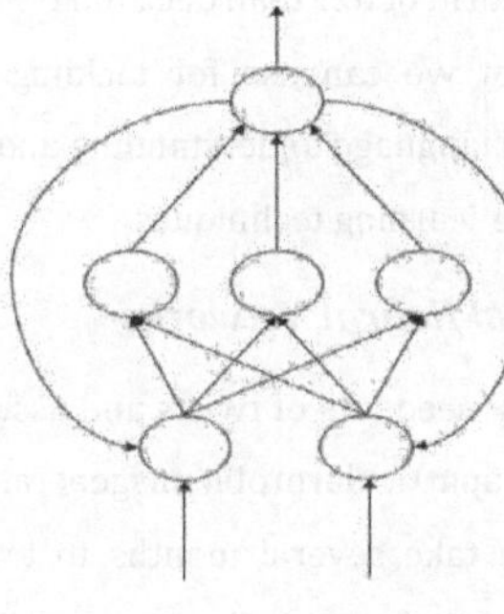

Figure 52: Feedback ANNs

Source:https://www.tutorialspoint.com/artificial_intelligence/artificial_intelligence_neural_networks.htm

5.3.2. Machine Learning's in ANNs

- SUPERVISEDTRAINING.
- UNSUPERVISEDTRAINING.

Supervised Training

Here, both the input and the output will be given. Then the ANNs will process the inputs and then it matches its resulting outputs with the desired output. If any error occurs, then it is sent back through the system, leads the system to adjust the weights that control the network. This process will continue till the weights are continuously fine tuned. The set of data which enables the training is called the "training set." While giving training of a network, the same set of data is operated many times till the connection weights are ever refined.

If the problem is not solved by the network, then the designer of ANNs has to review the input and outputs, the number of layers, the number of elements per layer, the connections between the layers, transfer, the summation, functions. Those changes required to create a successful network constitutes a process wherein the "art" of neural networking occurs.

Unsupervised

In this type of training, the network is provided with inputs, but not with desired outputs. The system itself must then decide what features it will use to group the input data. This is often referred to as self-organization or adoption.

5.3.3. Advantages of Artificial Neural Networks

- ANNs can easily understand complex representations. This is why, for example, in some cases ANNs can perform better than decision trees.
- ANNs are flexible so that we can use for tackling conventional Neural Networks (IMAGES), time series and language understanding and generation.
- They are used for machine-learning techniques.

5.3.4. Limitations of Artificial Neural Networks

- Neural Networks basically need lots of twists and assumptions, and selecting the right topologyormethodtosolveaparticularproblemisgenerallyconsideredasa black art.
- Neural networks literally take several months to train, whereas the decision trees training is easy because of their divide in nature and algorithms such as bagging and random forests can easily be parallelized. Artificial Neural Networks also can be parallelized but it is a complex process.

- Neural networks usually take a lot of time to evaluate than the decision trees takes less time, fast and powerful-efficient.
- Neural networks are not efficient in small datasets.

5.3.5. Applications of Artificial Neural Networks

Artificial neural networks are mostly used for

- Pattern classification.
- Clustering or categorization.
- Prediction/forecasting.
- Content-addressable memory.
- Optimization.
- Function approximation.

Text-to-Voice Translation

Here the input is given in text input by using the keyboard and then it is converted to NETalk pattern, then the NETalk pattern is sent to the NETalk Network. The Network converts the phoneme into an analog signal. Finally the input is translated into voice and it is heard via speaker.

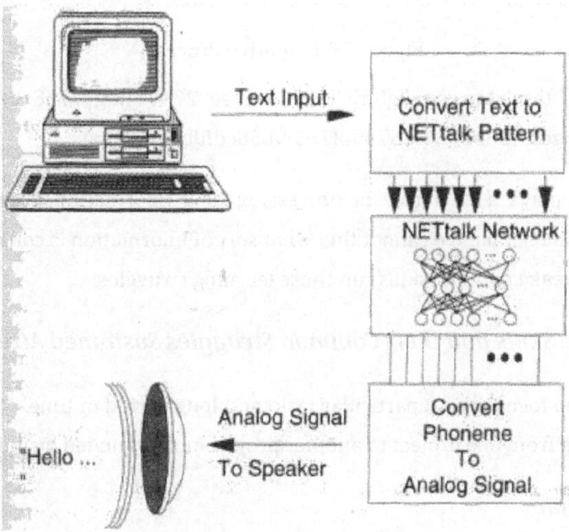

Figure 53: Text to Voice Translation

Source:https://www.tutorialspoint.com/artificial_intelligence/artificial_intelligence_neural_networks.htm.

5.4. Cognitive Reasoning

Cognitive skills involve brain to perform thinking, learning, to remember, reasoning and to pay attention.

By using these cognitive skills, we can use input information and perform according to that and send it to the bank of knowledge, as an output.

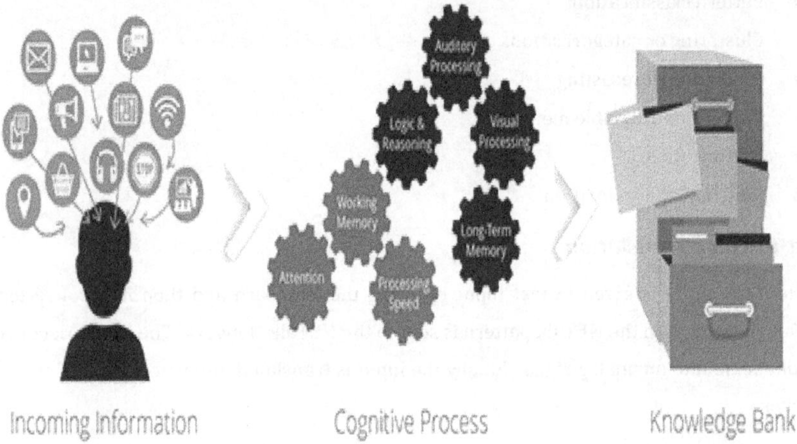

Figure 54: Cognitive Process

Source:https://fthmb.tqn.com/fgl_a77MF9H7_Lasox27bVTJIqg=/768x0/filters:no_upscale()/about/GettyImages-498637581-57b9bf7b5f9b58cdfdbd783b.jpg

Cognitive skill plays a vital role in processing new information because if any of the cognitive skills weaken, then we cannot find what sort of information is coming in our way and also one or more weak cognitive skills can cause learning struggles.

5.4.1. Cognitive Skills and their Common Struggles Sustained Attention

It allows to keep focused on a particular task for a long period of time. These skills may get weak when moving from one project to another project or surrounded by unfinished projects.

Selective Attention

It keeps to stay focused and enables to ignore distractions while doing a project. Selective attention skills may get weak when moving from task to task or when distracted easily.

Divided Attention

It allows to remember all the information when we do two things at a time. Divided attention skills may get weak when we make frequent mistakes or when not being able to do multiple tasks.

Auditory Processing

It helps to blend, analyze and segment sounds. It is a demanding skill for successful reading. This processing may get weak when we are having difficulty to read or learning or reading fluency or comprehension.

Visual Processing

It helps us to think the images in visual. This processing may get weak when struggling to understand what have read, remember what have read, follow directions, reading maps, doing word math problems.

Memory /Working

It keeps to hold tightly on information while are using the series of actions. The working skills may get weak when we have to read the directions once again during the project and also feel difficulties when following multi-step directions.

Memory/Long term

It helps to access, hold on to stored information that was learnt in the past. This skill may get weak include doing tests poorly, web forgetting names, forgetting things which we used to know.

Logic and Reasoning

Logic and reasoning allows to reason, form ideas, and solve problems. Signs that logic & reasoning skills may be weak include frequently asking "What do I do next?" or saying "I don't get this," struggling with math, feeling stuck or overwhelmed.

Processing Speed

Processing speed keeps to do tasks quickly and accurately. Signs that processing speed is weak include the ongoing feeling that doing tasks are more difficult for other people, taking a long time to finish tasks for school or work, always being the last one in a group to finish something. Because cognitive skills are so critical to each and every aspect of thinking, learning, and performing, weak skills should be addressed.

Cognitive testing measures exactly how each skill is performing, and gives a detailed look at which skills are strong and which are weak. If cognitive testing identifies one or more weak skills, cognitive training can target and strengthen those skills.

5.5. Natural Language Processing

Natural language processing (NLP) is the affiliation among computers and human language. More especially, NLP is the method in which computer is capable to recognize, analyze, and manipulate the technology of human speech (natural language).

The NLP denotes speech analysis in both audible speech, in addition to textual content of a language.

NLP structures describe the means from the input of phrases like sentences, paragraphs, pages, and so forth, in the shape of an ordered output that varies significantly depending on the application. Natural language processing is a fundamental element of artificial intelligence.

However, it is far more than simply speech evaluation, there are a whole lot of approaches for processing human language.

5.4.2. Approaches in Natural Language Processing

Symbolic Approach: It is totally based on human-developed policies and lexicons. The base behind this method is the common regulations of speech within a given language which can be materialized and recorded by linguistic specialists for PC structures to comply with.

Statistical Approach: It is based on observable and recurring examples of linguistic phenomena. The computer system can develop its own linguistic rules, so with the help of linguistic rules it can further investigate the future input and output.

Connectionist Approach: It is a combination of the symbolic and statistical approaches. It accepts the rules of language and adapts them to desired applications based on the input which is derived from statistical inference.

Ultimate Goal of NLP: The final intention of NLP is for computer systems to achieve human-like comprehension of texts/languages.

When the remaining intention is executed, the PC structures will be able to apprehend, draw inferences, summarize, translate and generate correct and natural human textual content and language.

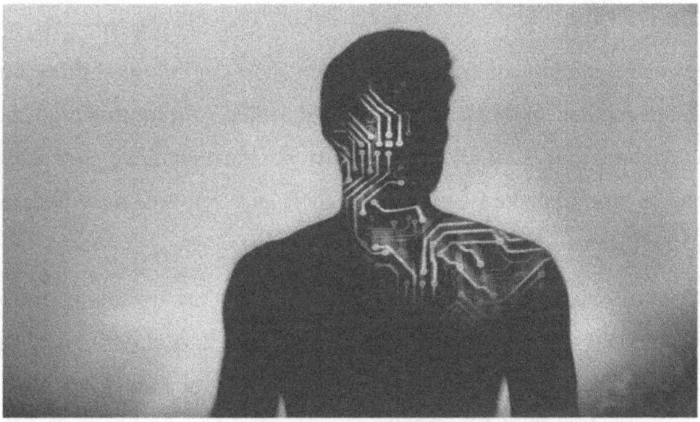

Figure 55: Natural Language Processing

Source:https://fthmb.tqn.com/fgl_a77MF9H7_Lasox27bVTJIqg=/768x0/filters:no_upscale()/about/GettyImages-498637581-57b9bf7b5f9b58cdfdbd783b.jpg

5.6. Cognitive Computing Algorithm Application

Machine Translation

As of now, all the information belonging to the world is available online, so the task to make these data available has turned out to be totally important. The challenge of making the world's information accessible to everyone, across language barriers, has simply outgrown the capacity for human translation.

However, machine translation offers an even more scalable alternative to harmonizing the world's information. The challenge with the machine translation is not in translating words, but in protecting the meaning of the sentences, a complex technological issue that is at the heart of NLP.

Fighting Spam

To fight against spam, the first level of defense that comes to mind is spam filters. But almost everyone who uses email extensively has experienced the agony over unwanted emails that are still received, or important emails that have been accidentally caught in the filter.

The false-positive and false-negative issues of spam filters are at the heart of NLP technology, again boiling down to the challenge of extracting meaning from strings of text. A technology that has received much attention filtering a statistical technique in which the incidence of words in an email is measured against its typical occurrence in a corpus of spam and non-spam emails.

Information Extraction

Many crucial decisions in economic markets are more and more shifting far from human oversight and management. Algorithmic buying and selling is becoming more popular, a form of financial investments that is totally managed by using technologies. However, a lot of those economic decisions are impacted by way of news, via journalism, which is still offered predominantly in English.

A predominant mission, then, of NLP has turned out to be taking those simple text announcements, and extracting the pertinent information in a format that may be factored into algorithmic trading selections. For example, news of a merger among agencies could have a massive impact on trading choices, and the speed at which the particulars of the merger, gamers, fees, who acquires who, can be incorporated right into a buying and selling set of rules, can have earnings implications inside the millions of rupees.

Summarization

Information over-burden is a genuine wonder in our computerized age, and as of now our entrance to learning and data far surpasses our ability to comprehend it. This is a trend that indicates no signal of slowing down, and so a capacity to summarize the meaning of documents and information is turning increasingly vital.

This is important no longer just in allowing us the ability to understand and take in the pertinent data from big amounts of data. Another desired outcome is to understand deeper emotional meanings, for example, based on aggregated data from social media, can an organization determine the overall sentiment for its contemporary product providing? This branch of NLP turns increasingly more beneficial as a treasured marketing asset.

Question Answering

Search engines positioned the world's wealth of records at our fingertips, but are nevertheless normally quite primitive in relation to virtually answering unique questions posed via people. Google has seen the frustration this has caused in users, who often need to try a number of different search results to find the answer they are looking for.

A big focus of Google's efforts in NLP has been to recognize natural language questions, extract the meaning, and provide the answer, and the evolution of Google's results page has shown this focus.

Though certainly improving, this remains a major challenge for search engines, and one of the main applications of Natural Language Processing research.

5.7. Social Neuroscience

Social Neuroscience is a term implemented to an emerging field of study concerned with identifying the neural procedures underlying social behavior/cognition. However, the sphere extends beyond a look for neuro chemicals and mind regions that motivate behavior. Social Neuroscience seeks to better understand the relationship between the brain and social behavior.

Social species are so characterized due to the fact they form agencies that amplify beyond the character. The purpose of social neuroscience is to investigate the biological mechanisms that underlie those social structures, processes, and behaviors and the influences between social and neural systems and techniques. Such an enterprise is hard as it necessitates the combination of multiple tiers. Mapping across structures and degrees from genome to social groups and cultures requires interdisciplinary information, comparative research, revolutionary strategies, and integrating conceptual evaluation.

5.7.1. Methods of Social Neuroscience

Contemporary social neuroscience makes use of a broad variety of methods that are often used in combination with the more traditional tools of social cognition. In addition to new technologies for measurement, Social Neuroscience methodology relies on the use of careful experimental designs, valid manipulations of psychological states and processes, and careful inference and interpretation. Here, we describe the most prominent methods currently used in the field and briefly discuss their relative advantages as they relate to experimental designs, issues of construct validity, and psychological inference. A more detailed description of methods in Neuroscience approaches to Social Psychology is provided by Harmon-Jones and Beer (2009).

Early studies take a Social Neuroscience approach primarily used for peripheral physiological methods, such as electrocardiogram (e.g., heart rate), galvanic skin response (i.e., skin conductance, a measure of sympathetic activation, and electromyography (e.g., measures of facial muscle activity related to emotional expressions). More recently, neuro imaging methods have become particularly important and, as such, tend to dominate in the literature. These techniques include functional magnetic resonance imaging (fMRI), which measures the flow of oxygenated blood in the brain, and electroencephalography (EEG), which measures electrical activity produced from the firing of neuron populations. EEG activity measured in response to a discrete event, such as a stimulus or subject response, is called an event-related potential (ERP). These methods differ in important and complementary ways.

MRI yields high-spatial resolution and that is optimal for determining the location of activity within the brain. But, because it assesses slow-moving blood flow, its temporal resolution is slow. By contrast, EEG/ERP yields high-temporal resolution and is thus optimal for assessing the timing.

5.7.2. Benefits of Social Neuroscience

The current excitement approximately has vast recognition of Social Neuroscience and it is grounded in a developing appreciation that it could benefit Social Psychology in a number of approaches. At first, some observers sometimes assume that Social Neuroscience simply tries to map social-psychological processes of activity in specific brain regions. Of course, this type of research exists. In fact, identifying neural correlates of psychological functions can sometimes be quite useful, as it can serve as a springboard for further theory-testing investigations (in addition to more anatomical benefits of brain mapping). On the other hand, the brain mapping of social processes is problematic. Theoretically, the "mapping sport" tends to supply an increasingly developing record of quite a lot of capabilities assigned to a unique discipline, with little benefit for research thinking about checking out psychological propositions. Happily, the study on neural correlates shouldn't be the one or the primary function of a neuroscience method to Social Psychology. Here is what we see as the proper benefits of Social Neuroscience.

First, neuro scientific studies and idea can tell theoretical debates in Social Psychology. In Cognitive Psychology, several theoretical debates have been substantially formed by using neuro scientific research (for example, debate approximately the character of imagery, shape of memory, early versus overdue attention choice). Similarly, in Social Psychology, Neuroscience information can make a contribution to such proof. As an example, do not forget studies with the aid of Amodio et al. (2004). Integrating ideas from Cognitive Neuroscience models of cognitive control (Carter et al., 1998; MacDonald, Cohen, Stenger, & Carter, 2000) with a brief overview of Social Neuroscience.

5.8. Synthetic Intelligence

Synthetic intelligence (SI), often referred to as engineered intelligence, is a refinement of the idea of synthetic intelligence (AI). SI acknowledges that although the capability of software program to reason can be manufactured, its miles despite the fact that real intelligence and not simply an imitation of ways people accumulate and observe knowledge and talent. Traditional packages of Synthetic Intelligence have frequently relied upon software that surely mimics human intelligence through replicating easy human thought procedures.

Haugel and refers to this technique as GOFAI (Good-Old Fashioned AI).SI software goes past simulation, taking benefit of the methods that machines gather and practice understanding and capabilities at each digital and mechanistic levels.

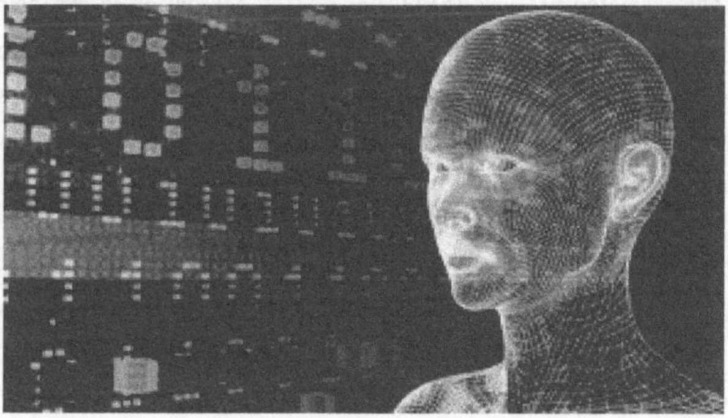

Figure 56: Synthetic Intelligence

Source:https://encrypted-tbn0.gstatic.com/images?q=tbn:ANd9GcRcZX12J9Gx-xREcc7qe4mg1k1n9Dv3FBpFK6SXc6m7K3kNHSToyg

5.8.1. Build Whole Functionalist Architectures

There are two aspects to that slogan: First, we are in need of functionalist architectures. That is, we need to make explicit what entities we are going to research, what constitutes these entities conceptually, and how we may capture these concepts. For instance, if we are going to research emotion, simply introducing a variable named "anger" or "pity" will not do. Rather, we will need to explain what exactly constitutes anger and pity within the system of a cognitive agent. We will - among other things - need to acknowledge that anger and pity have objects that require the perception and representation of (social) situations, and equip our model with these. We will have to capture that anger or pity has very different ways of affecting and modulating perception, learning, action selection and planning, memory and so on - and we have to depict these differences. To explicate concepts underlying intelligence and mind is to get away from essentialist intuitions (for instance the idea that emotion, personhood). In the sense that natural sciences assume that formal (i.e., computational) theories are adequate to capture their respective subject, the universe itself is a computational phenomenon. This is not a strong claim as it may seem to some, because it merely entails that the universe presents itself as information patterns to the systemic interface of the experimenter with his or her domain, and that these patterns are both necessary and sufficient for the experiment's measurement.

Normative behavior, consciousness and so on just are done by some module or correspond to some parameter, and to replace them with a functional structure that produces the set of phenomena that we associate with the respective concepts. Second, we need complete and integrated systems. Isolated properties will not do, for perception is intrinsically related to deliberation, a deliberation to emotion, emotion to motivation, motivation to learn and so on. The attempt to reduce the study of intelligence to a single aspect, such as reasoning or representation is like reducing the study of a car-engine to combustion, temperature fluctuations or rotational movement.

5.8.2. Avoid Methodologism

When we grow up to be AI researchers, we are equipped with the beautiful tools our Computer Science Departments have to offer, such as graph theory, binary, modal and fuzzy logic, description languages, statistical methods, learning paradigms, computational linguistics, and so on. As we discover the power of these tools, they tend to turn into the proverbial hammers that make everything look like a nail. Most AI researchers that abandoned the study of intelligence did not do so because they ran into difficulties along that course, but because they turned to some different (worthy) subject, like the study of graph-coloring, the improvement of databases, the design of programming languages, the optimization of internet agents, and the definition of ontologies. However, there is currently no reason to think that understanding intelligence will be a byproduct of proving the properties of our favorite description language, or the application of our favorite planner to a new domain of the funding agencies choosing. We will need to ask questions and find methods to answer them, instead of the other way around.

5.8.3. Aim for the Big Picture, Not the Individual Experiment

Our understanding of intelligence will have to be based on the integration of research in the cognitive sciences, possibly in a similar vein as the medieval and Renaissance map-makers had to draw on the data made available by travelers, tradesmen, geographers, geometers and explorers of their times. Just as these map-makers pieced together a map of the world from many sources of data, we will have to draw a map of cognition and the mind by integrating the knowledge of many disciplines. Our current world maps are not the result of choosing a small corner of a small village and improving the available measurements there, because these measurements are not going to add-up into an unified picture of geography (before that happens, the landscape is likely going to change so much as to make our measurements meaningless in the big picture.).

Our first proper maps were not patchworks of infinitesimally small measurements, but the product of gradual improvements of a big picture. Disciplines that are concerned with individual measurements often sport methodologies that are incompatible with sketching big pictures. Note that Albert Einstein did not do a single experiment whilst designing the theory of relativity -- instead, he noted and expressed the constraints presented by the data that was already available. Likewise, the study of AGI aims at an unified theory, and such a theory is going to be the product of integration rather than specialization. This point is likely a controversial one to make, since it seems to insinuate that the exploration of specific topics in AI is futile or irrelevant, which of course it not the case -- it is just unlikely to result in an understanding of general intelligence.

5.8.4. Build Grounded Systems, but do not Get Entangled in the Symbol Grounding Problem

Early AI systems tended to constrain themselves to micro-domains that could be sufficiently described using simple ontologies and binary predicate logics, or restricted themselves to hand-coded ontologies altogether. It turned out that these approaches did not scale to capturing richer and more heterogeneous domains, such as playing a game of soccer, navigating a crowded room, translating a novel and so on. This failure has opened many eyes to the symbol grounding problem, i.e., how to make symbols used by an AI system refer to the "proper meaning."

Because of the infinitude and heterogeneity of content that an intelligent system must be capable of handling to satisfy a multitude of conflicting and evolving demands (after all, intelligence is the answer to that problem), AI systems will have to be equipped with methods of autonomously making sense of their world, of finding and exploiting structure in their environment. AI systems will probably have to be perceptual symbol systems, as opposed to modal symbol systems, that is, the components of their representations will have to be spelled out in a language that captures the richness, fluidity, heterogeneity and orientation of perceptual and imaginary content.

5.8.5. Do Not Wait for the Rapture of Robotic Embodiment

It is fascinating to see a little robot stretching its legs. Eventually, though, the level of intelligence of a critter is not measured by the number of its extremities, but by its capabilities for representing, anticipating and acting on its environment, in other words, not by its brawns but by its brains. Insects may continue to rule the planet long after humankind has vanished, but that does not make them smarter than us.

There may be practical questions to build robots instead of virtual agents, but the robotics debate in AI is usually not about practicality: Unfortunately, a lot of research into AI robots is fueled by the strong sense of "meaning" originating in a Searle style conception of the Symbol Grounding problem. This sense of meaning, however, can itself not be grounded. For any intelligent system, whether a virtual software agent or a physically-embodied robot (including us humans), the environment presents itself as a set of dynamic patterns at the systemic interface (for instance, the sensory3 nerves).

5.8.6. Build Autonomous Systems

As important as it is to integrate perception, memory, reasoning and all the other faculties that an intelligent system employs to reach its goals, is integration of goal setting itself. General intelligence is not only the ability to reach a given goal (usually there is some very specialized but non-intelligent way to reach a singular fixed goal, such as winning a game of chess), but includes the setting of novel goals, and most important of all, about exploration. Human intelligence is the answer to living in a world that has to be negotiated to serve a multitude of conflicting demands. This makes it a good reason to believe that an environment with fixed tasks, scaled by an agent with pre-defined goals is not going to make a good benchmark problem for AGI.

5.9. Summary

- This Chapter discusses about the emerging evolution in cognitive computing application.
- Affective Computing is defined as the study and the development of the system and the device that can able to recognize, interpret, process and simulates the human effects.
- It describes about Artificial Neural Networks and their basic structure, types, advantages, disadvantages.
- It discusses about natural language processing, social neuroscience and synthetic intelligence and their structure, advantages and disadvantages.